SISTERS IN ARMS

Lessons We've Learned

Molly

Thank you for Inspiring Me,

Honored to know you,

God Bless

Deb Kielty Vhon

2023

SISTERS IN ARMS
Lessons We've Learned

Williamsburg, Virginia
www.BlueDragonPublishing.com
Copyright 2023 Dawn Brotherton
ISBN 978-1-939696-85-4
ISBN 978-1-939696-86-1 (epub)

Table of Contents

Foreword

Sandra Stosz
Vice Admiral, USCG, Retired

Sisters-in-Arms is a treasure trove of genuine stories told from the heart by veterans who served on the leading edge as women were integrated more fully into the armed forces following the Vietnam War. Although the history of women serving in certain roles extends back over 200 years, it was not until the twentieth century—during World War I—that women were allowed to openly serve in the military. At that time, women still didn't have the right to vote, and they were limited to support roles. During World War II, each branch of the armed forces stood up a women's reserve force. Women served in noncombat roles, yet many of them performed traditional male duties such as test piloting airplanes and maintaining machinery.

Those pioneering women paved the way for the women like me who joined the US Coast Guard when women began serving more broadly on active duty in the armed forces in the early 1970s. I entered the US Coast Guard Academy in 1978 with the third class to include women, and it was hard. Women made up 5 percent of the corps of 1,000 cadets, and we were often isolated in those early days. Some of the men scornfully declared that we didn't belong at the Academy and we weren't "real women." Talk about a blow to a fragile self-esteem! But the bond of sisterhood helped us survive and even thrive!

Dawn Brotherton, a twenty-eight-year Air Force veteran and published author, has curated a powerful collection of lessons learned from remarkable women who, like her, were often among the first women in their chosen fields. She continues to serve by elevating the voices of these brave women who blazed the trail—most often without recognition—for others to follow. These words are directed at women who are considering joining the armed forces or who have recently raised their right hand, but they are lessons we can all learn from.

Although these stories reflect the diversity of the authors' backgrounds and experiences in different branches of the armed forces, they share a common theme of resilience. Read how one woman who didn't know how to swim surprised her instructors with her grit and determination. Learn how another found the courage to stand up to men who tried to unfairly hold her to different standards. You'll be amazed at what some of these women endured and overcame in those early years.

In *Sisters-in-Arms*, you'll find inspiration learning how women thrived through challenging times by demonstrating courage and perseverance. You'll discover how each woman learned to believe in herself and harness her inner strength to achieve her goals—and how you can too. Don't let the stories told by these incredible women role models lie dormant; share them widely so that others may discover the courage and confidence to reach high and become the very best they can be!

Sandra L. Stosz
Falmouth, Massachusetts
Author, *Breaking Ice and Breaking Glass: Leading in Uncharted Waters*

Introduction

I was inspired to create this project during the 2022 Virginia Women Veterans Summit in Richmond, Virginia. During the conference, the Veteran Entrepreneur Investment Program Fund Operations Manager from the Peninsula Federal Credit Union asked a few of us to introduce our businesses. I was selected to pitch.

Blue Dragon Publishing's goal is to help make a writer's dream a reality by coaching publishing options and helping writers shape their story.

As fun as it was to address the 200 or more people at the event, I was amazed by the number of women who caught me afterward because they wanted to tell their story; they just had never thought it possible.

But I wanted to do more than just publish their short story; I wanted to teach them how to become an author and what that process entails.

I reached out to a wider audience through the Women Veterans Alliance (https://www.womenveteransalliance.com/) and invited writers from across the country to participate. We started with more than eighty writers who met online as small groups over a four-month period to review each other's drafts. As the reality set in on the effort it takes to write and publish a book, many dropped. Along the way, I offered webinars covering basic copy editing, publishing options, and writing tips.

A bonus along this journey was that women veterans from various services got to know each other better. As a result, empathy and respect for each other's trials and accomplishments developed, and friendships blossomed.

This project was three-fold. First, for the writers to tell their story. Second, for them to be encouraged to continue writing and publishing. And third, to inspire readers who are considering joining the armed forces or those who have just begun their journey. I want them to see how far women have come in the military, and how much further we still have to go.

Women have only been considered veterans for 75 years, after the signing of the Women's Armed Service Integration Act on June 12, 1948, by President Harry Truman. Integrating women wasn't easy, and there are still battles taking place. To arm for action, you must have the proper equipment and knowledge. Sharing our history is one piece of the puzzle.

Sisters in Arms: Lessons We've Learned was born.

Dawn Brotherton
Colonel, USAF, Retired
Author and President of Blue Dragon Publishing, LLC

A Leap of Faith

April E. Brown, Major, USMCR, Honorarily Retired
October 1985–April 1998

In 1993, United States Marine Corps Commandant General Carl E. Mundy stated on CBS *60 Minutes* that minority Marine officers "can't swim, shoot, or use a compass as well as their White counterparts." He went on to express regret and said he didn't mean to imply that Black officers were less capable.

Hearing these comments in the interviews on national news jolted me back to my swim qualification experience at The Basic School for Officers (TBS), seven years prior. As hurtful as these remarks were, I knew there was some truth to the Commandant's statement.

In December 1985, I was commissioned in the United States Marine Corps from Officer Candidate School (OCS) located at Marine Corps Base (MCB) Quantico in Quantico, Virginia. OCS was ten weeks of grueling training intended to eliminate the weak. The environment is designed to make you want to quit. The platoon sergeants and sergeant instructors use every physical, mental, and emotional tactic to highly encourage you to drop out. A candidate may be sent to an administrative board for low performance in academics, tactics, or the subjective category: leadership. The board determines if a candidate will continue at OCS.

My OCS platoon started with fifty-four women, and we commissioned fourteen at the end of ten weeks of training. Of these fourteen, I was the only Black woman to commission and was

9

one of forty-three Black female officers out of 240,000 active duty and reserve Marines.

After OCS, my next stop was TBS, located on the west side of MCB Quantico, nestled away from the main side, amid a large training area called Camp Barrett. Lieutenant General Frank E. Petersen, the first Black Marine Corps aviator and first Black general in USMC history, was the commanding general (CG) for MCB Quantico. As a Black officer, I understood the significance of this. Little did I know this would be the only time during my years of service that I would serve on a base whose CG was Black.

As a newly commissioned second lieutenant, I looked forward to learning how to lead Marines. OCS was meant to weed out candidates who weren't qualified to be officers. In TBS, I would learn military history, tactics, leadership, and how to take care of my Marines. I was ready to be mentored, supported, and pushed to high expectations. I was excited to embrace the challenge and enthusiastic about what was waiting for me at TBS.

Tactics, land navigation, history, and leadership were going well, but the swim qualifications was my Achilles heel.

When I joined the Marine Corps, I didn't know how to swim. I could go to a pool and splash water while holding on to the edge or jump in the deep end and "swim" back to the surface, but it wasn't really swimming. It was more like playing. Swimming was a requirement to be a Marine. Not researching this basic stipulation was an oversight on my part.

We marched from the bachelor officers' quarters to the water training facility. As we filed inside the building, I smelled the chlorine and saw the water in the massive pool. A twenty-foot tower stood at the far end. Our Water Safety Instructors told us to line up along the side of the pool. We were dressed in green t-shirts and camouflage utilities. Those of us who wore glasses or contacts were told to remove them. As I removed my glasses, I felt vulnerable. I couldn't see clearly; therefore, I couldn't hear as distinctly. Reading lips and observing body language was a natural part of communication for me.

After we lined up, Instructor Matthews directed all non- or weak swimmers to raise their hands. Of the approximately 200 lieutenants, about twenty raised their hands. I raised my hand, thinking we would be removed from participating and be taught how to swim. Nothing was further from the truth.

We were told to go to the front of the line and climb the steps to the top of the tower. This had to be a joke. We weren't going to be required to jump off the tower into the water if we couldn't swim. It's just a subtle form of harassment. The instructors wouldn't possibly make non-swimmers jump into water.

Oh, but they did.

When my turn came, I knew, despite my fear, I had to jump. The entire company of Marine lieutenants and the TBS instructors were observing our behavior. As a Black woman, I didn't want to have to represent my race or gender, but in this case, I was representing both. When you are the "only," you're always hypervisible. This was my reality. As the only Black female officer in my company at TBS, I was always visible in a very different way than my peers.

My platoon commander was on the tower with me, and I'm certain she saw the fear in my eyes. She gave me the slightest nod of encouragement. I locked my body, took a deep breath, and leapt off the tower before I could change my mind. I couldn't see clearly, so I had no idea when I would hit the water.

I jumped off that tower as if I knew I would suddenly become an Olympic swimmer through the magic of the Marine Corps. It was a shock to my body when I landed in the water. I sank but somehow floated back up to the surface. It's true, the Marine Corps is magical.

That was until I went back under.

As I went under the second time, panic set in. I gulped in water and thrashed about, trying to claw my way to the surface, which only made it worse. I knew I was drowning; I could feel it.

I heard someone saying, "Grab the pole. Grab the buoy!"

How could I grab something I couldn't see? I didn't have my glasses on.

I heard a splash and saw the outline of a body coming toward me.

Sergeant Jones said, "I got you; grab me."

I grabbed Sergeant Jones and wrapped my legs around his torso. Then I proceeded to try and use him as a ladder to climb out of the water. The next thing I remember was lying on my back on the cold tile with the instructors hovering over me.

Sergeant Jones yelled, "I'll let you drown before I try to save your ass again."

Apparently other instructors had to rescue Sergeant Jones from my headlock as I held him under water. Years of powerlifting had strengthened my legs—I could deadlift and squat more than 300 pounds. Plus my fear of letting go added to the equation. There was no way he was getting out of that headlock.

I earned quite the reputation with that move; the instructors had to knock me out to get me to release him. After that, I was known as the strong woman Marine, said with a semblance of respect by other officers.

Nicknames are often earned at TBS based on performance, an experience, a screw up, or other multiple reasons. Those of us who couldn't swim were known as the "rocks." Other lieutenants used this as a way to humiliate, mock, or play head games . . . all in the spirit of competition.

Each of the non-swimmers' experiences had become comedy for the lieutenants in the company. Some second lieutenants pretended to drown and shouted out "Rock!" when they passed an unqualified swimmer. They retold the stories of how we couldn't swim and how one of the Haitian Foreign Military Officers refused to jump and claimed the United States was trying to kill him. The insult of being called a rock in an environment that is highly competitive was not lost on any of us. Subjective peer evaluations were often based on reputation, and those evaluations determined our ranking in the company. This may not seem significant, but TBS peer evaluations often determined future promotions. No one wanted to be in the bottom.

To graduate from TBS, every lieutenant must pass swim qualifications. There were four levels during the time I was at TBS. S3 was the minimum qualification. A lieutenant had to jump and swim to the side of the pool with any type of swim stroke. This included the dog paddle, which most new swimmers used. All the formerly unqualified lieutenants eventually accomplished this. The other levels were S2, S1, and Water Safety Qualified (WSQ). Each level was progressively harder with WSQ being the highest. To pass S2 and S1, I was required to learn the breast stroke, the side stroke, and any form of back stroke and swim the length of the pool using each stroke. S1 had the same requirements as S2, but it also required an underwater swim the length of the pool. During the underwater swim, I could only come up one time for air. The underwater swim was the most difficult part for me.

To earn WSQ, I would have to jump off the tower and turn my camouflage utilities into a flotation device by pushing air into them, remove my boots, put them on top of the flotation device—all while making certain my rifle stayed on my shoulder—and then tread water for an hour. Daunting, yes; impossible, no. This was my goal!

Years later, I came to understand that this practice of grading was a reflection of an unlevel playing field. If you came from a community where there was access to swimming pools, you probably learned how to swim. If you didn't have access to a swimming pool, you probably couldn't swim. It didn't mean you couldn't learn; it just meant that access was limited in your life experience.

I was determined to show my peers I had the grit to perform at the highest level. All I needed was the instruction and opportunity.

The pool was open in the evening for lieutenants who had not passed swim qualifications. Those of us who failed the first attempt were required to go to the pool until we at least passed the lowest level of S3.

I was determined to pass my basic swim qualification within a week, and I did. The percentage score for S3 equates to 70 percent. When a lieutenant does not qualify on their first attempt of swim qualification, the highest score they can earn, regardless of the level achieved, is 70 percent. In other words, the minimum score.

Having now passed the S3 requirement, I had no obligation to continue swim remediation or attain a higher level. Attaining a higher level would not improve my score of 70 percent. The scoring at TBS used the first score obtained, regardless of the level achieved later.

Even though I knew my score wouldn't increase, I asked one of my instructors, Master Gunnery Sergeant Washington, if he would work with me to attain a level higher than S3. My goal was to show my peers that my background didn't determine what I could achieve, and quite frankly, I didn't like only meeting the minimum standards. Master Gunnery Sergeant Washington agreed to help.

Swim instruction took place in the evenings, after a full day of second lieutenant training. It also meant I had to give up dinner and evening social time with my peers. During the next four months, I went to the pool, usually from 1800 hours until about 2000 hours every evening. After swimming, I had to wash, condition, and straighten my hair, which took about two hours. I fixed a snack, studied before going to bed, then got up to start the next day of training.

The first evening I arrived, Master Gunnery Sergeant Washington was waiting and seemed surprised I had actually shown up. I was in awe of this Black Marine who was not only a "Master Guns" (the highest enlisted rank in the Corps) but was also one of the top swim instructors.

Master Gunnery Sergeant Washington had deduced my main issue was a fear of water. I'm certain he observed me flinch when water splashed on my face or panic when I felt like I was struggling in the water. I didn't like the vulnerability of being in the water and not being in control. I always thought of water as dangerous, the enemy, something to avoid.

He was patient and thorough. On the first day of training, he helped me establish a relationship with the water as my friend. As I sat underwater, he spoke to me. "You're good. Relax. Slowly come out of the water. Now go back down."

I practiced this for an hour and learned to enjoy the solitude of being underwater, leaving behind all the stress and distractions of the day. My fear of water began to dissipate, and I was astounded how much difference this made. I moved to the next step of learning the actual techniques of swim strokes.

Some of my peers who struggled with passing the basic

requirement didn't understand why I continued to come to the pool when I didn't have to. Some senior officers asked the same question. One of the reasons I continued was because of Master Gunnery Sergeant Washington. I trusted him, admired him, and viewed him as a mentor. He was part of a culture and community I was missing.

There were times I felt isolated, alone, and marginalized by my peers. I had not found this type of support, sense of belonging, or connection until now. Subconsciously, maybe I didn't want to let him down. After all, he was taking his personal time to assist me. I also recognized he was an *only*: the only Black swim instructor at TBS. There was an unspoken bond we never talked about, but we knew existed. He believed in me, and it gave me strength to accomplish the goal I set.

After three weeks, I obtained the S2 qualification. S2 equates to 80 percent of the test score. Master Gunnery Sergeant Washington reiterated that even though I had obtained a higher rating, my score would still remain at 70 percent because my first attempt when I jumped off the tower had been graded as a failure. He asked if I wanted to continue. For me, this was more about my personal goal and less about the score itself. I had something to prove to myself and others.

As I prepared for the S1 level, a few senior company platoon commanders from TBS showed up at the pool. Apparently, word had traveled about what I was trying to do. The senior officers rooted for me when I dove into the water. They offered encouragement as I mastered the techniques required for the breast stroke, the side stroke, and the back stroke. One captain yelled, "You can do it, Lieutenant Brown!"

Another officer gave me tips on my underwater swim. "Use your muscular legs to push off as hard as you can, and that will help you travel underwater."

I'm certain some officers were also curious about this relationship between a Black, senior enlisted man and a young, Black, female second lieutenant.

Eventually, even the lieutenants who were still trying to pass the swim qualifications cheered me on. I hoped my presence inspired them in some minute way to achieve their goals. I continued to go to the pool and eventually achieved the WSQ level, but my records would always reflect a 70 percent on the test. I was okay with that, because this was for me and Master Gunnery Sergeant Washington.

Earning WSQ was not without consequence. While I was improving my swimming techniques, my female peers were meeting for dinner each evening. During this time, they shared stories, bonded, and developed relationships with each other. My absence was interpreted as not wanting to engage with them.

I felt marginalized by the other female lieutenants. They couldn't understand why it was important for me to prove to myself, my command, and my mentor that I could pass my qualifications. I was not included in conversations that focused on women Marines, but when anything was mentioned about race, the subject was changed or I was asked to validate my experience.

A few of the female second lieutenants complained to my platoon commander, Captain Bloom. She informed the company commander that she was concerned about me not making an effort to fit in.

This was largely because I was not at the social dinner hour with the other female lieutenants in my platoon. I'm certain her personal experience as a female, prior-enlisted officer gave her insight on how important it was to be seen as one of the team.

The company commander, Major Alexander, called me in and asked about my behavior. I explained to him what I was doing each evening.

"Have you shared this with your platoon commander?" he asked.

"No, sir."

"Sometimes you'll have to toot your own horn and make yourself visible."

I struggled with this concept because I was not doing this for accolades, but I valued the lesson from Major Alexander. As a Black Marine, he shared ways I could be successful, even when I may not be *seen* as successful. He said that my experience would have an intersection of race and gender that many of my peers would not have to think about.

Major Alexander subsequently talked with my platoon commander. Some say he admonished her for not asking me about my absence.

After this incident, I felt distanced from Captain Bloom. I wanted her mentorship, guidance, and support. I also wanted her to know me and not just what was on the surface. I often wondered why she listened to the other lieutenants but never spoke with me directly before going to Major Alexander. I missed having a sense of belonging and community. I hadn't anticipated how lonely it would be as the only Black female in my company.

But I learned a very valuable lesson and will never forget my swim qualification experience. I looked fear in the eye and took the plunge. I survived. I pressed myself to be better. I didn't let my peers determine my worth, and I wouldn't let an institutional policy prevent me from achieving what I knew I could do.

I never formally thanked Master Gunnery Sergeant Washington for his coaching, mentorship, and support, but I hope I honored his teaching by supporting and guiding other Marines.

The Marine Corps motto is *Semper Fidelis*, Latin for "Always Faithful." I'm reminded by this motto to be faithful to what you know you can accomplish, even in the midst of adversity.

April Brown has worked in higher education for over thirty years. She serves as the director of veterans' services at Texas Christian University, is a board member on the non-profit organization Hearts2Heal, and co-edited Voices of America: Veterans and Military Members Tell Their Own Stories.

The Rappel Tower of Terror

Kimberly L. Munguia, Major, US Army, Retired
January 1991–August 2021

"Come on, Jackson!" Drill Sergeant Zamora yelled.

"Damn it, he's seen me," I thought.

Zamora, a lean Puerto Rican man, was one of the best drill sergeants in the battalion, and none of us in the platoon ever wanted to let him down. He was fair yet stern, a no-nonsense kind of guy. We saw the alternative, and the other drills seemed mean to their soldiers. A female drill sergeant even hit one of her soldiers; at least, that was the rumor. I didn't understand how each platoon thought their drill sergeant was the best when it was obvious Drill Sergeant Zamora was head and shoulders above the others.

Drill Sergeant Zamora must have seen how I hesitated and wanted to climb back down the rappel tower. Why else would he call out my name? If I backed out now, after being seen, not only would I pay, but the entire platoon would have to do push-ups, and everyone would hate me for bringing the pain. And worse, I would have let down our good drill sergeant.

The day started out like every other day in Army Basic Training. We got up at oh-dark-thirty (about four thirty in the morning), dressed, did our personal hygiene, and cleaned the open bay barracks where the sixty or so of us females lived, laughed, and at times, cried. We were all between the ages of seventeen and thirty-two years old. I was eighteen at the time.

It was a cool February morning in 1991 at Fort Jackson, South Carolina. On this day, our platoon marched like a well-oiled machine to the dining facility. We were in week two of basic training and knew just what to do. When we arrived, we dutifully withdrew our "Smart Books" from our left cargo pant pockets and began studying them.

"Who is the secretary of the Army?" my buddy quizzed.

But I didn't pay attention to her; I was too busy dreading what was to come in just a few short hours. We were going to the rappel tower. A rappel tower is a monumental tower to climb up and then rappel down, or in other words, hurl yourself over the side of. At most basic training locations, such as at Fort Jackson, they are about forty feet high, but some are over seventy feet tall. The Army calls these confidence courses, because they're supposed to build your courage and let you know that you are capable of great accomplishments.

I hate heights. Growing up, I was so petrified that I refused to climb even the shortest of trees. Just jumping over the fence in our backyard to go to school freaked me out to the point of near tears. How in the heck was I going to scale down the side of a forty-foot structure? Just the thought made me sweat.

The student platoon leader piped up from behind our platoon. "Put away your smart books and prepare for chow."

"Platoon. Atten-shun!" yelled the student platoon sergeant.

Outside of the dining facility, sixty of us snapped to attention, bringing our feet together and hands straight to our sides.

"Left, face," bellowed the student platoon sergeant. "File from the right, column right."

The four squad leaders turned their heads. Three called out to their squads, "Stand fast."

Simultaneously, the fourth squad leader repeated, "Column right. March." The squads disappeared a few soldiers at a time beyond the door and into the feeding line.

I was in second squad, so it was going to be a bit before I got to eat. I was okay with that; I was already feeling the nerves causing the pit in my stomach to turn just thinking about what lay ahead after chow. I pictured myself tossing up chunks of pancakes and eggs all over those who dared to stand below me at the tower.

After breakfast, we began the long march to Jenkins Road where the forty-foot monster known as Victory Tower was located. Our student platoon sergeant called soldiers out one at a time to take up their position and call cadence. Cadence is pretty much the same thing as the repeat-after-me songs that we sang in Girl Scouts or at school and church camps. It's used to keep us all in step, so we look disciplined and professional—and also so we don't trip over the person in front of us. I loved calling cadence, because I have always loved singing, and this was just like singing but with a captive audience. Cadence starts when your left foot hits the ground.

The first soldier sang, "They say that in the Army the pay is mighty fine."

Fifty-nine female voices echoed back as loudly as we could. "They say that in the Army the pay is mighty fine."

"They give you a hundred dollars and take back ninety-nine," she called.

Again, we echoed it. The singing helped take my mind off what we were about to do.

The woodsy scent of pine was strong in my lungs as we marched past the huge pine and sycamore trees that kept the looming tower just out of sight. We turned the corner to the left and there it was. The forty-foot tower of doom stood right in front of me. I counted the platforms in my head: one, two, three, four, FIVE! My stomach immediately sank, and I could no longer think, much less yell out in singing glory. The girl next to me elbowed me to keep singing, but I couldn't. My throat felt like it was closing in, and I suddenly felt nauseous and dizzy. Good thing I didn't eat the eggs at breakfast. I didn't feel like tossing myself from a four-story building today—or any day for that matter.

We came to a halt a few hundred feet from the monstrosity and were instructed to drink water out of our canteens while Drill Sergeant Zamora went to find the rappel master. They returned shortly and the rappel master instructed us to sit in a U-shape, so we could see and hear her instructions. Then, she went over what was to happen. We were going to put on what was called a "Swiss Seat," climb that beast to the top, grab a rope, and jump down the side wall.

I began sweating again and worried that my hands would be too wet to keep my leather gloves on.

I was having a hard time paying attention to her instructions because of the bees buzzing around in my head. The rappel master must have seen my face turn pale.

"Look, I know this looks big, and some of you are afraid of heights."

Was she talking to me?

"But we've got you, and you've got this," she reassured. "Your drill sergeants and my team do this all the time. We will not let anyone get hurt, but you're going to have to dig deep and muster up the courage to get to the top of that tower. Privates, this is the Army, and you must learn to overcome your fears. That's called personal courage, and it's what wins wars."

"Okay," I thought. "I can do this. I have courage. I can win wars."

I was trying hard to convince myself, but it wasn't working. The pit was still in my stomach. The rappel master finished showing us what to do. She showed us how to tie a Swiss Seat and on-belay and off-belay the rope.

Then it was time. The music played in my head, "Beethoven's Fifth" or was it "Chopin's Funeral March"? Yes, "Chopin's Funeral March" from his *Piano Sonata No. 2* played over and over in my head as I inched closer and closer to the behemoth that was taking my soul away. But I didn't seem to be getting any closer; instead, that thing just kept getting bigger and bigger until I was standing at the bottom, looking straight up into the sky.

"Okay, it's my turn. You've got this, Jackson," I tried to coax myself. "Win wars. You're in the Army. You're brave. You can do this. It's almost over." Wait, what?

What was I telling myself? Why would I use the word over when I was about to hurl myself off the side of a wooden building that was bigger than anything I had ever been in, or on, before? I let others go in front of me, while I tried to muster up the courage. Slowly, I climbed the stairs to the first platform. *That wasn't so bad now, was it?* I thought.

Then I got to the second platform. "Okay, you've got this; keep going."

Then the third came, and the nerves boiled up again. I hesitated but kept going. I got to the fourth, then I made a huge mistake. I looked back at my platoon on the ground, and it was all over for me. I started shaking. They looked so small down there and so very far away.

I was about to turn around and go back down. Surely, they hadn't seen me, so no one would know that I didn't rappel. They would all just assume that I had, and that I was joining them afterward like everyone else. We were there with five other platoons anyway, all intermixed and going through at the same time. Who could tell that, out of about 300 troops, I was the one who hadn't gone? That's when I heard him.

"Come on, Jackson!" Drill Sergeant Zamora yelled.

Damn it, he's seen me. Too late. I begrudgingly made my way to the last platform—the dreaded top.

I compelled myself to take the last step. The wind pushed the tower from side to side, and I almost lost my footing. I visualized myself being thrust through the air by the wind and over the side to my death below. I couldn't move another inch.

A male sergeant sat on the far edge of the platform, his feet precariously dangling over the side, motioning for me to move forward to his position.

"Come on, Private!" he yelled. "Let's go!"

It wasn't a mean yell, just loud because the wind up that high was blowing hard. I inched over to him, crawling on my hands and knees, and quickly took a seat. He helped me get into position with my feet now dangling over the edge of the forty-foot wall.

I took a big breath in. Then I got onto the board that stuck out from all the rest. I took in another really exaggerated breath and blew it out as slowly as I could to calm my nerves. I was to put my left arm out front, stiff, with the rope in my hand, while my right arm was bent behind me in the small of my back to control my descent and not just drop to the bottom.

That's when I almost died.

He told me to lean back. Lean back? Over what? He wanted me to sit on thin air with my legs locked in front of me, my butt hanging out over the world and the ground below?

His stern words reassured me. "I'm here. You will not fall, Private. I will not let you fall. Now sit back."

I did.

"Okay, good, now take a step down to the next board."

I did this too, but it took me by surprise as I had forgotten I was on the board that stuck out farther than the others. I almost went too far backward but caught myself with my right hand by controlling the slack in the rope. My hands shook inside the leather gloves, and I was dizzy.

"Good reflexes," the sergeant said. "Now get comfortable with it. Remember, you're in control of your destiny, not the tower. Jump in place a little bit, Private."

I didn't want to, but I did it. It was surprisingly comforting, not bad at all. I jumped a few more times in place, and each time, my feet found the wall with relative ease.

"Okay," he said. "You're doing good. Can you believe the Army actually pays you to have this kind of fun?"

I let out a little giggle and shook my head no.

"Now, time to get off my tower, Private. Let out more slack and jump."

I descended a few feet, and again, my feet found the wall. This was starting to be fun. I did it again and again, each time letting out more slack from the rope, and each time going a bit faster and further down the side. By the time I got to the ground, I was ecstatic! It was so much fun!

But I was okay with not going again, at least not that day. The soldier on the ground helped me off-belay and get out of my Swiss Seat. I was still glad I hadn't eaten eggs that morning.

I trotted over to where my platoon waited. Trembling in the aftermath but so proud of my accomplishment, I reported to Drill Sergeant Zamora.

"Yes, Drill Sergeant?" I asked.

"Yes what, Private?" he returned.

"I heard you call me when I was on the tower. Did you want to see me?"

"Private, I didn't call your name. Now get in formation so we can leave," he said.

What? He hadn't called my name? Had I just made it up? And I went down that horrendous tower? I could have fainted right then, but I was still high on my sense of accomplishment.

On the march back to the barracks, I again couldn't call cadence. This time though, it wasn't because I was scared or nervous. It was because I was in awe, yet again, about how the Army showed me that I was capable of doing things that I had thought were impossible. That I should never again limit myself by thinking that I can't do something. I'm capable of doing so much more. We all are.

We just need to not allow our minds to talk us out of it.

Kimberly Munguia has returned to her love of writing and tries to write daily. She's looking forward to one day becoming a screenwriter and documentary filmmaker. She lives in rural California with her wonderful family of four humans, two doggos, three cats, and several chickens.

Lessons From Hollywood

Dr. Angela Karnes Padron, Staff Sergeant, USAF
January 2000–January 2007

He burst into the room. "What the hell has been going on with you?"

I could hardly look at him as tears swelled. I tried to muster my military bearing, but the last eighteen months had taken their toll on me. I let the tears stream.

That was the day I first met Master Sergeant Michael Beckett.

I grew up in Indiana, surrounded by cornfields and big dreams. My dad was a dreamer; my brother was a dreamer; and I was a dreamer. Working at McDonald's in high school paid all right. I moved up quickly to crew trainer and then manager—not bad for a seventeen-year-old.

Work and school became an escape. I found an eclectic boyfriend at school who was edgy enough to feel like I was rebelling. Things with Matt started to get serious. He became more appealing the more my parents despised him. I ran away three times throughout high school. The third and most dramatic time, Matt came to get me. It was a bit of a knight-on-a-white-horse situation through my young, troubled eyes. This runaway attempt was my most successful as well. I made it four states away in a couple of weeks before I ran out of money and had to call Matt to come get me.

Soon after we returned, life settled into its unsettled state living with my family—I missed my period. I didn't think much of it but

25

bought a home pregnancy test anyway. I took the test, hid away in the bathroom, and still seated on my throne, watched the plastic, my leg bouncing. I'm only seventeen!

I slowly walked out of the bathroom, met Matt's eyes, and extended my hand with the test toward him.

He laid down on the cold, hardwood floor and stared at the ceiling. "There's twenty dollars in my pocket. Go get a box of tests."

I was on delayed enlistment with the Army for eighteen months during high school. The plan was for the military to be my way out of a difficult homelife, but more importantly, my ticket to the world.

When I told my Army recruiter I was pregnant, he was angry to lose his recruitment number. I lost my spot.

I was destined to be a statistic—a teenage mother. A few months later, Matt and I went to the city courthouse with a handful of our high school friends and family and shared vows two weeks before I graduated high school.

When the smell of eggs made me sick, I quit my job as the morning manager at McDonalds. Matt worked part-time at Blockbuster Video. We found ourselves moving toward becoming another statistic. We were not only teenage parents, but now we were members of the "living on food stamps and welfare" club. We had a ration of a block of cheese, a loaf of bread, a jar of peanut butter, a gallon of milk, and baby formula each week. This was a long way from my dreams of far-off places.

I was much more submissive then but wanted more for my life. I finally convinced Matt to let me join the military. I didn't know anyone who had been in the military at that point. I had not grown up with grandfathers as war vets. I had Hollywood's take on the military and being a part of the Air Force was nothing like Demi Moore in *GI Jane* or Goldie Hawn in *Private Benjamin*. I believed Hollywood and the recruiters who benefitted from my enlistment. I knew it would be a huge leap of faith to join, but faith is what I needed to carve out a promising future for my son.

At the recruiting station, I decided to see what the Air Force offered our little family.

Boot camp was tough. Not seeing my husband and son was tougher. Early in my Air Force career, I had a setback. My first supervisor, Staff Sergeant Barker taught me my first leadership lesson: don't be like her.

I had been home for two weeks from a deployment to Saudi Arabia when the 9/11 attack happened. A few days later, I reported to Andersen Air Force Base, Guam, in support of a new mission. Only my supervisor and I were from the Operations Resource Management (1C0X2) career field, and we joined a few dozen airmen from our base in different fields like aircraft maintenance, medical, life support, and administration.

Barker and I alternated from midnight to noon and noon to midnight; I worked the latter shift. About ten days into our deployment, I got to my shift, and she asked me to take a seat. She had a white piece of paper in front of her that looked official. She tossed the paper in my direction.

"Here. Sign this."

I glanced over it quickly.

"I didn't ask you to read it. I said sign it," she barked.

I caught the title of the form: LETTER OF COUNSELING (LOC). I had heard of the form but didn't quite know what it was. I had also skimmed the words "rental vehicle off-post" and "without my consent."

I immediately responded, "Ma'am, I didn't take any vehicle off-post. I only use it to go to our dorm, here, and the dining facility."

She again said, "Just sign it."

My hand was shaking, my heart was pounding, and I felt tears around my eyes as I signed it. I wasn't sure what the LOC would do to my career.

Over the next week, I asked other airmen how an LOC could impact my career, and the consensus seemed to be it would affect future promotions for up to five years. I was a dutiful and driven airman, and this was devastating. It would prevent me from commissioning to officer and hold me up for a while. If there was something for me to take responsibility for, I would have, but I hardly understood the accusation. I wasn't responsible for the things she was saying so I couldn't correct my actions.

Still in a haze of confusion, I stood in the humidity of my Guamanian pseudo-paradise outside of Burger King on a payphone. It was time for my call home to talk to Matt and my son. This call was different.

When I greeted Matt, he said, "I got a call earlier from Sergeant Barker, and she said you're sleeping around out there."

My breathing stopped when his words hit me.

I tried to explain. "She's lying! She's lying about this, and she made up a story she gave me paperwork about last week."

This was now confirmation that she was sabotaging me. I started to share the story of the paperwork she gave me.

He said, "I don't care about military matters right now."

"But it isn't true. I'm trying to handle things here. You have to believe me! Everything she said was a lie."

I heard a click.

When I got to work, Staff Sergeant Barker was sitting at our desk with another form. *There's no way that I'm signing another piece of paperwork.* I was livid from the call with Matt and now this.

She didn't insist that I sit this time. She simply set the paper in front of me. "Sign it."

It had been a week since I signed the first LOC, and this one was the same form and mentioned the rental car and off-post but seemed like an escalation about wasted fuel and specific mileage amounts. Was she tracking me now?

Thinking of the call with Matt, I said, "Ma'am, I didn't do this. I didn't do this last week either. I sure didn't do what you told my husband. I've been cheated on before, and I would *never* do that to someone."

With no hesitation, Staff Sergeant Barker rose from her seat and, with tight lips and tense jaw, slowly whispered inches from my face, "You will sign this, or I will have your son taken away from you."

Why is she doing this? Can she do that? Does she really have that much power?

My fury was now gone. Crushed with fear and holding back tears, I reached for the pen. I scribbled letters on the form. She snatched it the moment my pen left the paper. The imminent threat of terrorist attacks was nothing compared to the ultimatum just thrust on me. I went to the first sergeant to share my concerns. He knew "Toni" well and said that she had already shared what was going on. He dismissed me entirely.

Matt took our son to Portland, Oregon. Two weeks later, I was served the divorce papers. I found myself not eating or sleeping. My only comforts were smoking cigars and talking with a few friends. One night I was standing outside my hangar smoking and looking at the beautiful night sky when I realized my hand was shaking so much that I needed both hands to steady the cigar enough to reach my mouth. This was the lowest point of my life.

Our unit returned to my home station of Fairchild Air Force Base, Washington, on a sunny Friday. I looked out at a sea of flags and signs and heard cheers of joy. My squadron commander was at the bottom of the stairs shaking hands with everyone as they hopped off the plane and onto American soil. When it was my turn, he didn't extend his hand.

He looked me in the eyes. "You start alert duty on Monday. Be there at twenty-three hundred hours."

I was devastated by the lies that followed me home. I was to pick up my son the next day and had until Monday to figure out daycare for him from eleven at night until eleven in the morning, six days a week. Others got two weeks at home with their families. Not me.

I was disappointed. We were taught to act with integrity, honor, and respect. I was in love with the Air Force, but I found myself marking giant Xs on calendars waiting for the end of my enlistment just like I had done when I was seventeen waiting for my eighteenth birthday.

Months later, after my return from alert duty, we learned Staff Sergeant Barker was eight months pregnant. No one had noticed because she often wore a large Gortex jacket, even in the warm months.

A month later, she told everyone that she lost the baby at birth. Hearts were breaking for her, including mine. That's a horrible thing to happen to anyone. She spoke of the funeral and burial and had accepted gifts and food from everyone around her. Within a few months, she moved to a higher-level position as a technical sergeant on base to finish her military career. This meant a new supervisor for me.

Master Sergeant Mike Beckett stood waiting for an answer while my thoughts scrambled to decide whether to be honest with my new boss. I decided to open up some and take one last shot at sharing my side.

I mustered my voice. "Those rumors are not true at all—none of it."

I could barely catch the words as they spilled out. I didn't have much else to lose, but I knew I was at risk by speaking about Barker, a non-commissioned officer. The quiet void was eating away at me.

He sat down, relaxed in his chair, and said three magical words that all leaders should keep in their toolkit. "I believe you."

Stunned for a moment, I blurted out, "You do?"

He brushed off the shock and disbelief I displayed and said, "Yeah, that sounds like Toni. I've known her for a long time."

It was incredible! Immediately the weight lifted. I was given my voice and my humanity back in a matter of seconds. I went on to share the whole story.

He said we would work on my reputation together but also explained that Toni, as he referred to her, could be very convincing. He left our meeting with reassuring words. "I know this has been hard. I'm asking you to trust the process."

I walked back to my desk and tore up my countdown calendar as a sort of personal reenlistment ceremony.

The contrast between my two supervisors taught me many lessons. I learned the power that one person can have on another. I learned the true meaning of leadership and the importance of having a voice. Master Sergeant Beckett gave me that. He wasn't just my supervisor; he was my leader.

Under his leadership I found myself doing well. I tested for promotion, and I made staff sergeant. It turned out Barker couldn't do permanent damage to my career.

I was seeing my son 50 percent of the time, two weeks on and two weeks off. I received the distinguished graduate award in my sergeant school, and shortly after pinning on staff sergeant, I was leading my own team. I made it a point to lead with integrity and honor and treat them with dignity and respect. I met with each of them separately often to ensure they had a voice and felt heard. I knew I could either treat them the way I had been treated by Barker or do better.

Several months had passed when I got news that Technical Sergeant Barker decided to retire from her position at the headquarters after being there less than a year and was on terminal leave, the time before you're officially retired but not at work, so I didn't have to see her around base anymore either.

A month later, Master Sergeant Beckett said they needed a bailiff for a court-martial trial, and I was qualified if I was interested. Immediate thoughts of *People's Court* episodes ran through my mind.

"It could be fun, sure."

He grinned slightly.

The day of the trial came. I received an inbrief on the responsibilities of the bailiff, and that got my adrenaline going. What if this is a huge person? How can I tackle them? Scenarios danced in my mind, but it was exciting and new. I took my position near the door, stood at parade rest, and waited attentively.

The jurors and attendees filed to their seats. This was a small base, and I recognized several faces in the crowd. Master Sergeant Beckett and my commander were there. *Hmm, where did the commander find the time to attend these things?*

The prosecutors entered and took their seats on the right, and I watched the door to be sure the accused didn't act out as they entered.

It felt like several minutes went by. A suited man came in first with a sharp, spikey haircut. I thought he might've overdone it on the gel for such an occasion. A woman shuffled a few feet behind him. I glanced at her outfit She wore a forest green, long sleeved, turtleneck shirt with a light tan and plaid vest, and a long, black pencil skirt. I didn't care for the outfit. She looked like a schoolteacher trying too hard, but when my eyes reached her shoes, I appreciated those. They had curved heels and reminded me of what a stereotypical witch would wear. *A schoolteacher witch.* I chuckled to myself.

She looked down while walking to her spot, and her hair fell messily over her eyes. There was something familiar about her though. I examined her thoroughly; she was my objective after all. She must've felt my stare, and she broke her hunched posture to glance my way. I caught her eye and gasped. I caught myself and popped back to my parade rest stance and serious face.

Is that Barker? It looked like her, but I wasn't sure. My eyes were the only mobile thing on my body, and I explored the room. Master Sergeant Beckett caught my eye from across the room. I used every bit of energy to communicate through them and keep still. He answered my nonverbal question with a gentle smile and nod. My jaw gaped open. He gestured with a finger to his jaw. I smiled and closed my mouth.

My mind was running a million miles a minute. My heart pounded in my chest, and I felt warmth swarm my body, starting on my back.

She saw me. Does Barker know it's me as well? Did Master Sergeant Beckett have something to do with this? He said trust the process. I told myself to pay attention to the courtroom and ask my questions later. This took great effort until the accusations came out.

Barker was accused of selling her government laptop; the JAG found it at a local pawn shop. The payment receipt appeared on the screen. I knew that handwriting. She had also fraudulently signed off on her out-processing checklist. She had signed the names for the different agencies around the base. Some of those folks were in the room as a picture of the checklist with false signatures appeared on the screen. This created some shifting and tension.

When asked to respond, she started her tearful lying. I had seen this several times before and imagined her winning an award for best actress. My father called those crocodile tears. No wonder so many believed her tales: the ones about me, the ones about herself, and everyone in between. She was sharing a sob story about her kids and needing to care for them. I thought about how she instigated my divorce and threatened my son. She didn't care about my family.

The prosecutors refuted Barker's character plea with more evidence. Directing the court to the display screen again, one said, "She speaks of being a family person. You'll see on the screen a string of emails."

They had accumulated twenty-three pages of emails between Technical Sergeant Barker and a senior airman stationed in Kansas.

Then the prosecutor zoomed in on a fancy PowerPoint timeline showing Barker's deployment dates and compared the dates to her relationship with the airman. The emails began immediately following her return. The prosecutor scrolled to the email string that discussed her pregnancy and revealed the correlation with the deployment dates.

She turned to the judge and the jurors. "This proves that Technical Sergeant Barker committed adultery during her deployment in the months of October through December 2001 based on her pregnancy."

My mouth fell open again. This time I caught myself and glanced at Master Sergeant Beckett. He gave another reassuring nod. Tears formed behind my eyes. I saw the motive. I understood why she had worked so hard to destroy my life. She needed a scapegoat. She needed the leaders to focus on me while she continued to do what she was doing. *Wow, it finally makes sense.*

I fought back the tears and checked back into the courtroom and out of my head. JAG moved to a later string of emails and said that Barker had given their baby up for adoption to a couple in California. The prosecutor highlighted a message Barker wrote to the airman stating, "I told them it died. They bought it."

The prosecutor went on to tell the court, "The emails between them after that were fewer and further apart."

The prosecutor's closing comments were, "So, you see, ladies and gentlemen of the court, judge, and jury, Technical Sergeant Barker is not the remorseful family woman looking to provide for her children. She was adulterous and deceitful. Your honor, I move to add adultery to the list of charges."

The judge nodded, and the prosecutor grabbed a folder on the table and handed it to him. The court recessed for an hour, and everyone marched out of the room. I stood at my perch until the room was empty. My heart had been pounding, and I realized I might've been holding my breath as I felt lightheaded and dizzy. On my own now, I let it out: my gasp and my tears. I slumped to the ground with weak knees.

A few minutes later, Master Sergeant Beckett opened the courtroom door. "I hate to interrupt, but do you have a minute?"

Immediate relief hit me as I ran to him and gave him a hug. Public displays of affection are not allowed except for certain situations like redeployment, military ceremonies, and funerals. This was not a typical situation. As I released my hug, I said, "Did you do this?"

He smiled. "I said trust the process. There are good people out there who wanted to do the right thing. It took a small army (fake coughs) or an Air Force to achieve."

Wow!

He had shown me that the core values of the military do exist, and people have integrity and honor. I explained that when he told me he believed me, he gave me my voice and instilled my hope in leaders again.

There are exceptions in every facet of life, and because Barker was so much the exception to the golden rule, we were sitting in that courtroom. I have used the mantra "trust the process" countless times since.

We continued to talk, and the hour was almost up as folks started entering the courtroom again. Everyone sat where they were before, but the room felt entirely different, or was it me?

I felt different. This was transformative. I took my post once more. The prosecutors came in, followed by the defense and then Barker. This time she didn't glance my way. I felt her shame and guilt as her arm lightly brushed mine coming through the door. She was sentenced to lose her E-6 rank and reduced to E-2 permanently. She also got two months additional jail time in Spokane. Her lies didn't work this time.

As soon as the gavel hit the wood, the courtroom started to clear again. This time my commander came by. "You're relieved of your post. Let's talk."

He pulled me to a side room in the building. "I'm sorry I didn't know. I'm very sorry. I didn't make this easier on you, and I will do better next time."

He asked for a hug. I knew this was more for him than for me; I obliged. I was vindicated, and I felt his honor and respect for me was restored. We were two equals with different ranks and responsibilities. I was a human, and I was respected again.

I spent seven years on a remarkable roller coaster of adventures, lessons in life, and leadership before being medically discharged. My service set me and my family on a beautiful path. I felt redeemed in my career and had my son half of the time, while Matt lived within driving distance. I met a wonderful man later in life. We married, and he supports my passion for the military and commitment to paying back the community that has given me so much.

I am eternally grateful for my decision to join the military and for this community.

Dr. Angela Karnes Padron is an organizational psychologist with the Department of Defense. She owns a consulting and staffing business, Olympus Strategies, which focuses on culture and change management, leadership and coaching, and project management. She enjoys her time with her loving husband and two beautiful sons.

Bras and Bytes in Biloxi: 1983

Reinetta Vaneendenburg, Captain, USN, Retired
August 1979–September 2016

"Lieutenant Van, see Major Shire after class," directed the instructor.

Uh-oh. It's never good to be singled out, especially when a student at a military school like Keesler Air Force Base in Biloxi, Mississippi.

As the Navy's equivalent to an Air Force captain, I was the senior person in the Air Force's "Introduction to Data Processing Course," Class 78. Unfortunately, I held the opposite position in academic standing. Learning how to program in COBOL and Assembly Language was kicking my butt. My classmates were not only junior, first-tour officers and younger (twenty-two to my twenty-six), they had studied computer science in college, which was just becoming mainstream in 1983.

I shrugged when classmates asked me what was going on when we filed out minutes later. I promised to tell them over lunch and ran up the stairs to the staff floor.

The brass plaque on the door read: Major S. I. Shire, USAF, Department Head.

The title was followed by a slew of Air Force acronyms I still couldn't decode a third of the way into this three-month course. Major Shire was responsible for the computer systems program, its cadre of instructors, as well as the hundred or so students cycling through the curriculum. I was the sole khaki dot in a sea of Air Force blue.

I knocked on the door and entered at the major's greeting. I was struck by the room's disarray, which was noticeably worse than when I checked in with him only last month. The office was sparsely furnished but still managed to look cluttered. A stock Air Force poster of an F-15 Eagle tactical fighter jet zooming through the clouds, its paper ends curling with age, hung behind a metal desk. A bookcase tilted behind a ratty couch, bursting with black binders and stacks of computer punch cards and printouts.

"Major Shire, you wanted to see me?" I asked.

The large, open box by the desk was new. It contained food, including the iconic ramen noodles and cans of soup of those living alone. A brown-tipped, spider plant in a Piggly Wiggly yogurt container tried to grow, despite being on the windowsill above a radiator. The room reflected the casual attitude the major displayed by his own appearance.

"Sure, Lieutenant Van, take a seat." He pointed to the lone gray metal chair with books stacked on it across from his cluttered desk. "Just put those on, uh, on the floor. How's it going?"

"Well, it's a challenge but doable," I said.

"Good. We don't get many Navy types here."

No kidding. If he were my sailor, I would jack him up for hair that was too long—way out of regs—and a less-than-fresh—okay, wrinkled—uniform. This was in sharp contrast to the spit-and-polish of the other Air Force officers in the schoolhouse, who always appeared inspection-ready. The scuttlebutt was that Major Shire was going through a divorce and that he slept here, in his office.

"I noticed. And you wanted to see me, sir . . ."

"Right. There's a problem in your class you need to take care of."

"What sort of problem?" The students were well mannered, nearly catatonic by Navy standards. Everyone seemed to get along. The top student was Air Force Second Lieutenant Davenport, a svelte Black woman we nicknamed "Ace" because of her technical acumen. I relied on her to decode the gobbledygook instructor-speak that would otherwise be over my head.

"It's a matter that requires a measure of delicacy," he hedged, chewing on a nail. "It seems that one of the students is consistently out of uniform."

"Tell him to get with the program," I said.

"It's not a he; it's a she." He twirled a glossy blue Montblanc pen. "I mean, the officer in question is a female."

"Then tell her to get with the program."

His polite cough was followed by, "Excuse me. We can't really do that. That's why you need to."

"Major, I'm missing class time that I can't spare. Tell me in simple terms that even a sailor can understand what the problem is and what you want me to do about it."

He stood up. "I had better close the door."

I hadn't heard of any disciplinary infractions among my cohort. I'd seen unsavory behavior after two Navy tours—heck, some of it was my own —so nefarious acts of all sorts were flying through my head, from drunk and disorderly to murder. What could warrant this attention, especially from Major Shire, who was way up the chain-of-command from the students and instructors?

"It's about . . . a . . . brassiere," he choked out.

At my smirk, he continued. "Second Lieutenant Davenport wears . . . a black one."

"You called me to discuss Ace's underwear?" I laughed. "Oh, you Air Force types are too much." I resisted using the nickname "Chair Force," but only just barely.

He put both hands on the desk and leaned forward as if to share a secret. "You must take this seriously. She wears a black . . . brassiere."

"And I wear a white one. And they're called bras, Major. At least since, oh, the 1930s."

Shire's face was crimson. "That's just it, she wears a black—one—and it shows through her uniform. Through the light blue material."

I started to laugh, then thought for a minute: less than 10 percent of the American active-duty military forces were women in 1983. Everything about "those girls" was new and not necessarily welcomed. Regulations for women's uniforms were seen as one more thing to keep track of and often passed on to the nearest woman to intercede. Like now.

"Sir, how did she respond when you pointed out this . . . discrepancy . . . to her?"

"Oh no, I—we haven't. We couldn't. That's why you need to. You must counsel her about the correct . . . one and the required correction."

"You're saying, Major, that one of your students has to change the color of her bra when wearing the Air Force blue shirt? And I'm the one to tell her?"

"Blouse, it's called a blouse for females and shirt for men. But, in a word, yes."

"Use your Air Force chain-of-command to—"

He shook his head before I finished the sentence.

Shire came from behind the desk and leaned against it, crossing his arms over his spreading middle. "You need to talk to her because you're both girls."

I stood up from the rickety chair to meet his gaze. A retort died on my lips. I knew it was a lost cause.

Just like among civilians, a junior's response to a senior's tasking or correction is either yes or no. The Navy's hearty "aye, aye" indicates compliance and may include questions about its execution. However, in the Navy, and I think across all the services, the junior has only one chance to state reasons for refusal. If the senior agrees with the junior's argument, then the matter or tasking is closed. However, if the senior does not agree, the junior cannot engage in point-and-counterpoint debate with the senior. It was, as my father used to say too often, "end of discussion."

"I'll talk to her today, Major. Give her a pay day or two, in case she needs to buy new, appropriately colored bras. They can be pricey." My sarcasm was lost on him.

Major Shire blushed again. "Oh, I wouldn't know."

You're telling me, I thought.

Later that night, I visited Second Lieutenant Davenport, who lived one floor above me in the base's officers' quarters.

"Seriously? The major couldn't even say bra?" Ace asked. She and I had a good laugh about the situation. We talked about other challenges of being minorities in the military over the Coronas I brought to assuage the reason for my visit.

Ace reached for another beer. "The guys treat me like a china doll that might break at the first difficult tasking—even though I know the systems better than they do—or a doormat to be stepped on. They send a woman to talk to me if there's any issue. Like they sent you. It's happened before."

"I tell you, Ace, I had to think a minute about this color stuff. I'm White and I wear a white or nude bra under the Navy shirts that are white or tan. But a black bra if it's under a black top, say our winter blues or civilian clothes."

Ace laughed. "I've been counseled to wear a black bra too."

"With this uniform? Oh no, so what do you do?"

She took a sip of the beer and stretched. "Whatever they want. I don't care; I just want to do my job."

I nodded. "The men have got to get over this. I was sure the Air Force would get human relations right, but obviously, we're all still learning. I tell the guys to just treat women like sisters."

Ace agreed. "It's not that hard. My three brothers were great. Mom insisted on us showing everyone respect. But they sure did tease me. And you?"

"My brother was more of a hitter than a teaser."

Ace patted my hand. "That's rough. Didn't your parents stop it?"

I shook my head. "No one would believe me, even when I showed them my arm's black-and-blue mark the size of an orange from his punches. What could I do? I was the youngest, and my brother could do no wrong."

Ace thought for a moment. "How about in the Navy?"

I shrugged. "I thought I was the only one getting hit on until I asked another officer. She was just promoted to lieutenant and had similar encounters with senior officers, officers in her chain-of-command, peers, and even enlisted. Neither of us reported anything. What good would it do?"

"Yeah, I know," Ace said. "My previous command railroaded a

woman—only on her first tour—for speaking out, and I don't want it to happen to me. My career is too important."

"Me too," I said. "It's still bogus, even with the Navy trying some convoluted system for reporting. How can they ensure our safety from sexual predators? The men know they can get away with it and they do."

Ace said, "Like the wolf guarding the hen house. But women hit on me too. In some ways, that's even worse."

I told her about being invited, with a very physical gesture, to join a three-way with a woman officer who was senior to me and a sailor while I was in Hawaii for training. "I laughed it off, saying they had the wrong guy. Nothing more was said about it."

I told her about attending Tailhook, the annual Las Vegas drunk fest for Naval aviators, and having a relaxing time. "I didn't drink a lot or stay out late with the fly boys. I hung out by the pool with a woman pilot who was my friend."

I told her about the executive officer repeatedly haranguing me to drink with him—and who knows what else he had in mind. The guy was my boss. Who could I ask to intercede? Finally I went to the base chaplain and explained the conundrum. "I told the chaplain that the only way to my room at the Bachelors Quarters was to pass by its bar. The executive officer was there every day after work, shouting at me to join him for 'just one drink.'"

Ace took a sip of beer. "Did the chaplain help?"

I shook my head. "That man of the cloth put his hand on my thigh and suggested we have an affair."

Ace was dumbfounded. "The chaplain said to sleep with him so your boss would back off?"

"Yeah, I don't know how having sex with him was supposed to solve anything. Get this. Both guys were married with kids. Twice my age. Fat. Today I can laugh about it, but it wasn't funny then. Everyone was senior to me. There was no one to turn to. I mean if the minister wouldn't even help me . . ."

The saying "Rank has its privileges" has been traditionally acknowledged, but it should never include ill-treating others, especially those junior who have been put in their charge for safety and professional development.

We talked about a few other strategies and agreed there wasn't much we could do to help other women; there were too few of us. However, it was a relief discovering that others had similar experiences, like the three situations that I had shared. On that note, I said goodnight, relieved my counseling an Air Force officer for uniform discrepancies had been successfully completed. And a friendship started.

Years later, I still think those Air Force officers abdicated leadership by skirting what were clearly uncomfortable topics by not enforcing standards across the board. Granted, much was going on in that post-Vietnam military era and sending women officers hither-and-yon without adequate preparation added to the stress and confusion of a society in flux. The other services weren't above reproach either.

When I wore the Navy uniform, men often told me to "jack up" a female about a uniform violation. Their rationale was a version of "I don't really know their regs, so you take care of it," or "it's better if it comes from another woman."

Then there was the classic, "I wouldn't know what to say." This was from a senior officer.

I've heard others up and down the ranks cop this attitude. They thought they were being sensitive to the differences between the sexes by not directly addressing such "feminine" topics as appearance in uniform or weight.

Truth be told, I usually complied with the request to intercede, certainly if it was a direct order from a senior officer. Not so much if the request was from a peer or out of my chain-of-command. Those men were surprised when I countered with, "You're responsible to know and enforce uniform regulations for women as well as men." Or the curter, "You take care of it. She's as much your sailor as your men are."

Things are better now, forty years later, with legal and systemic reforms that have more clearly delineated appropriate behavior and consequences for those who deviate from that standard. However, anyone familiar with the news has seen coverage of the on-going skirmishes as men continue to resist accepting women and minorities into what has traditionally been an all-male environment. It's also been challenging for women and minorities to express leadership styles that are effective, neither overly harsh nor indulgent.

These are some lessons learned that might help keep a young person out of hot water:

- Control the situation. No one gets in trouble Sunday morning on the way to church. Bad things happen when a person is drunk, it's late, and friends have left you and the area.
- Trust your instincts. If staying late with that supervisor to finish up a few details gives you the willlies, then find a tactful way around it, such as including a co-worker to join you or re-scheduling it for a workday when others are around.
- Mind your own business. Involvement in gossip can generate a world of recriminations and anger. Matters such as who is sleeping with whom should not be your business. I tried to stay out of interceding about the uniform discrepancy by focusing on the course and what I could control.

My account shows a few of the many ways that teamwork is important. Cooperation and respect are required for an effective sports team, class project, or family outing. My classmates were concerned when I was called "upstairs." Ace helped other students with the technical curriculum. I thought about how to best approach Ace and followed long-standing advice to "praise in public, correct in private." She and I spoke as equals as we reflected on our military experiences, understanding such details would remain between us. We shared the commitment to "do our jobs," which is the ultimate goal for those in or out of uniform.

National Endowment for the Arts Military Veteran Fellow Reinetta Van is a regular contributor to The War Horse. *The essay collection* Navy Blues: Between WAVES and Warriors *is under consideration for publishing. The oral history* US Navy Women Line Officers: From Support to Spear Tip *is under contract. The limited-edition* Armed Forces Staff College Fifty-Year Commemorative History *was published in 1996.*

We Were Simply Soldiers

Sue Rushford, Specialist 5, US Army
August 1979–July 1985

I recently had the pleasure and honor to attend a luncheon for fellow female veterans. The room was full of vivacious women. On my right sat a woman who was the last of the WACs (Women's Army Corps); on my left, a woman who was the first of the female soldiers after the WAC disbanded in 1978. I enlisted in 1979, when the Army no longer distinguished between male and female soldiers. We were simply soldiers.

We received the same training, did the same jobs, and received the same pay. Although logistically integrated, the concept of women training and serving with men was a new one and not always accepted. We encroached upon the last bastion of the world's biggest boys' club. I'm fortunate to have come out of it unscathed.

We were trailblazers. We didn't burn our bras, shout from rooftops, participate in demonstrations, or intentionally set out to break glass ceilings. We quietly put on uniforms and showed the world that we could, and should, serve our country alongside our male counterparts. We were simply soldiers.

To get there, however, was no small feat. Basic training, even when you're eighteen, is grueling. Our company consisted of one platoon of fifty women and two platoons with one hundred men each. During our marches, the tallest men were in front, setting the stride (out of meanness, I assume)—a stride impossible for shorter women to keep up without getting shin splints.

45

Tenacity and pride kept me marching through the pain. There were many other constraints that female soldiers had to climb over, crawl under, push through, and outwit. The obstacle course was not made for soldiers only five feet tall. One obstacle was level upon level, as if we were climbing up an apartment building with no walls. I couldn't even reach the next level, let alone pull myself up. Before I knew it, my compatriots pulled me up by my arms.

If you've ever wondered why veterans are considered community leaders, why school districts are seeking veterans to fill the teacher shortage, why veterans are self-disciplined and self-motivated—even those of us who have not seen combat—I point to the gas chamber exercise.

We marched into the free-standing, cinder-block hut wearing our gas masks. I knew the room was filled with tear gas, and I was excited but scared. When I got inside, I thought, *It's not so bad.*

On command, we took our masks off, yelling out our names and ranks. Unfathomable and terrifying are the only words I have to describe what it's like to breathe where there's no oxygen. After what seemed like an eternity but was probably only seconds, we filed out of the gas chamber like robots. We had been warned that if anyone rushed the exit, we wouldn't get out until we could do so orderly. Once outside, my eyes and nose ran uncontrollably. I couldn't see through my tears. I tried to breathe through my mouth, but it was full of saliva.

The drill sergeants screamed at us to run. Running creates a wind to get the particles of gas off clothing. Imagine the sight of soldiers running wildly, blindly, arms flailing, faces covered in snot and tears and drool. The exercise was a success! That rubber facemask contraption earned my respect and confidence.

Digging foxholes was another training exercise. While out on bivouac, we were tasked with mastering this basic soldiering skill. There was an immediate need of below-ground protection because we were expecting to be gassed in the middle of the night; the foxholes were a place for us to avoid the gas.

Despite the tenacity, the women couldn't dig nearly as fast nor as well as the men. Pride was not our motivator; it was the pragmatic matter of the gas that worried us. We did what we could and worked in pairs, conjuring up plans and checking on each other's progress. We laid down in our extremely shallow foxholes, fitting our bodies like puzzle pieces. Much to our relief, we were not woken up from our sleep and gassed, but we would have been ready. By collaborating, we were a force to be reckoned with. Brain over brawn. We were simply soldiers.

As hard as basic training was for men, it was harder for women. The drill sergeants made some—but very few—accommodations for us: allowing an ever-so-slightly decreased number of push-ups, turning a blind eye at the obstacle course, and passing a few of us (yes, including me!) even though we couldn't throw a grenade a safe distance.

In 1979, they were still trying to figure it out. Female soldiers had just started wearing fatigue uniforms (until then, they had only been issued dress and physical training uniforms). Now we were training with men. We were right there on the ground next to them, doing push-ups, ad nauseam. We were simply soldiers.

The women in my platoon earned the respect of not only ourselves, but the 200 men in our company. I knew there would be at least 200 men in the world who would never doubt a woman's ability.

Our blood, sweat, and tears, alongside the men, made us all soldiers.

Dedicated to Major Jayme Casgrain-Guido (1961-2001) who was immeasurably inspirational in her short life. We were Army privates together. After her enlistment concluded, she joined ROTC and rose to the rank of major in the Massachusetts National Guard. She belonged to that special breed of people whose support improved the lives of all those around her.

Sue Rushford owns Sue Rushford Editorial Services. She is an avid baker, much to the delight of friends and family. Her goal is to live within the Arctic Circle.

Don't Ever Quit

Mary Baker, Master Sergeant, USAF, Retired
January 1989–February 2013

I still remember lying on the ground. Doug, my brother, stood over me. Nine years my senior, he was twice as big as I was and three times stronger. I was just a puny four-year-old. I tried several techniques of rolling one way then another, even trying to crawl between his legs, in a futile effort to get up, but it was useless. He was a budding teenager and feeling his oats as he picked on me that summer afternoon in our yard under the maple trees.

So I quit. I quit trying.

I hoped my brother would tire of this game and move on to something sportier, like shooting squirrels with his BB gun or riding our minibike around the farm. But nope, he was not having it. When he sensed I was giving up, he straddled over me and poked his dirty index finger in my face. "No way!" he yelled. "You don't stop! You don't give up! You find a way to get up! You find a way to beat me!"

For a split second, I saw a glimmer of real love in his eyes, though I'm not sure he realized it at that moment. His bidding made me think, maybe, just maybe, there was a way for me to do it. I sighed extra loudly as I laid my head back on the ground. He raised up, put his hands on his hips, and taunted me. "Well?"

That was my chance to make a move.

I executed a forward somersault under his legs, rolling behind him. Jumping to my feet, I ran like my life depended on it, which it probably did. Finally, I beat him at his own game. Rounding the corner of our house, I looked back over my shoulder and saw him still standing there. My brother, with his best shit-eating grin across his face, rooted in place, shaking his head. I wasn't sure if he was annoyingly surprised or proud of me for getting away so quickly after his little inspirational talk. Either way, I kept on running, just to be safe.

A couple decades later, I found myself lying on the ground, curled up in my sleeping bag with my poncho as a tent, and I really did not want to get up. It was April in the Cascade Mountains of Washington, and I was at USAF SERE School. SERE is the Air Force's Survival, Evasion, Resistance, and Escape training that all aircrew members are required to pass to become a flier. It had snowed again during the night; a fact I discovered when I had to pee at three o'clock in the morning. I guess I was staying well hydrated.

I prayed time would stand still, and I could get a little more rest before our instructor barked at us to get up. The hikes were so strenuous in the snow and mud that I wondered how many more days of training I could make it through.

Just eleven months prior, I had undergone knee surgery to repair a wicked anterior cruciate ligament tear that happened during a softball game. I saw my dream of flying as a boom operator on the KC-135R tanker pass before my eyes as I lay on the operating table, and the doctor said, "Don't worry, we'll fix you up like new."

And they did. Six months later, the flight doctor cleared me to attend boom operator training at Castle Air Force Base (AFB) in Merced, California, followed by SERE training at Fairchild AFB in Washington.

Snuggled up in my warm sleeping bag, I heard the instructor milling around our camp. I squeezed my eyes closed even tighter as if that would stop the seconds from clicking forward on my Ironman watch when I heard a voice say, "Don't give up."

My eyes shot open as I looked around and held my breath. "You find a way. Get up and get going."

I sat up, peeked under the edge of my poncho, and looked outside at the camp. Our instructor was on the other side of the campfire, and no one else was up yet.

"Don't give up," the voice quipped again.

Geez, I was losing it already, and we hadn't even been through the "advanced beatings" and interrogation training yet. Instantly my mind flashed back to that hot summer day at home when my brother had me pinned to the ground. I smiled a bit, almost laughing.

"Very funny brother," I muttered, as I slipped cargo pants over my long johns in the sleeping bag. "I'm getting up all right."

As I laced my boots, I thought about the night before when we had decided to set up camp. The lieutenant in our squad thought it was a good idea for the enlisted airmen to gather firewood while he changed his wet socks to dry ones. I suggested that he could help us so we could get the fire going faster. To which he reminded me that, as a lieutenant, he outranked a staff sergeant, and perhaps I should do what I was told.

I deliberately sat down on a log to change my socks too, and he lost it, becoming completely unglued. He stood over me, yelling, "I said the airmen need to go gather firewood."

I retorted, "I agree. All airmen should gather firewood—officers and enlisted! I will gladly do this task if you join us."

He refused . . . and so did I.

I instructed the three other airmen to sit down and change their socks, appealing to the commonsense mentality of "all for one and one for all."

When they dropped their rucks, the lieutenant turned to them, screaming a full octave higher, "I said to get the firewood first!"

I rose from the log. "Let's all get firewood together."

The lieutenant spun around as our SERE instructor stepped in between us. "How about we do a little training this evening?" the instructor said. "There will be times while evading the enemy that you can't light a fire, so you need to know how to adapt to all types of situations, especially ones where you don't have any firewood."

That night in the field, we ate cold rations and other items that didn't require a fire for cooking. We also found out that cold air can dry socks, just not as fast as a good, warm fire.

The instructor pulled the lieutenant and me aside separately to discuss the situation, but I was not backing down on this one; I knew I was right. We were all in this together, or we weren't. The lieutenant refused to speak to me the rest of the night, which was fine by me.

A few days later, we found ourselves in solitary confinement cells during the prisoner of war and resistance portion of SERE training. "Enemy soldiers" (a.k.a. our instructors) "easily caught" us in the mountains and bused us to our prisoner of war (POW) holding camp. The rules of engagement had been previously explained to us. Now we were at a point in training where we had no clue what day it was or how long we had been awake.

One thing I did know: I could not stand at attention any longer in my solitary cell as we had been ordered to do by our captors. I was in some pretty good pain from being on my weakened knee for hours on end. Even though the doctor had cleared me for training, I was far from completely healed and not back to 100 percent. As quietly as I could, I sat down in my cell, risking being caught and getting the crap beat out of me—again.

I have no idea how long I had been sitting on the floor when the guard suddenly ripped open the door and yanked me out of my cell. He threw me into the center of the room where I could see dozens of doors just like mine. The lights in the corridor were so bright, a sharp contrast to the hours of darkness we had experienced in solitary confinement. I kept my head down until my eyes adjusted, acting as submissive as I could.

The guard screamed loudly for dramatic effect, ensuring all my fellow POWs in the other cells heard of my transgressions as well. I tried to explain to him I was tired, we were all tired, and I couldn't keep standing without food, water, and rest. I really needed to rest. We all needed to rest.

I'm sure he noticed my armband that bore a code that translated to my left knee being bad. Instead of beating me up, like I fully expected, he pulled my lieutenant out of his cell and began beating him because I wouldn't stand at attention anymore.

The guard made the lieutenant do all sorts of crazy stuff, up and down the corridor, walking like a donkey on all fours. Every time he went by me, the lieutenant hissed, "Just do what they're telling you to do. Give in, bitch! Just quit!"

"No, I'm not quitting," I snarled back as he slithered by. I certainly wasn't going to promise anything to him, or even the guard, that I couldn't realistically do. Besides, I was sitting and resting. Why should I give in now? After a short time, a phone rang at the end of the corridor. Annoyed by the interruption, our guard answered it, speaking in a hushed tone. The lieutenant cursed at me some more and ordered me to just give in.

"No way," I told him. "You're the one getting your ass kicked, not me. I'm enjoying this part of training."

"Fuck you, bitch," he cursed under his breath as the guard stomped back across the room toward us.

The guard yanked me off the floor, drug me down the corridor to the phone, and told me to explain to the camp commandant why my sorry ass couldn't stand at attention anymore. My hand shook and my voice cracked as I put the phone to my ear. "Yes, sir?"

"You know you are a prisoner, and you must do as you are told," the commandant said.

"But we're tired. We haven't eaten since we were captured. We've had limited water. We need to rest." My voice sounded weak. "Maybe I could stand more if I had food and water and some rest. We all need to rest."

The guard grabbed the phone from my hands and pushed me back to the center of the room and my buddy—the lieutenant.

After hanging up the phone, the guard threw us both back in our solitary cells and ordered us to stand at attention—or else. The inside of the cell was especially dark now because my eyes had been exposed to so much light. I thought I was dreaming when we heard the camp commandant say over the loudspeaker that we could all sit in our cells for a while. There was a collective sigh from our whole group as we slid down the walls to the floor and curled up to rest on the cold pavement. Finally, we could rest.

I didn't give up that day. I didn't quit. Over the years, I learned there's a time and a place to fight your way back up or to stay on the ground. During my career, there would be many more opportunities for me to either stop and stay still or find a way to fight and get back up. Discerning when it was the right time to do each has not always been easy.

Many times, I defaulted to the fight mode, battling my way along in my career, scrapping to assert myself and get treated fairly as a female aircrew member. Other times I was so tired of fighting, I just wanted to lie down and quit. When that happened, I heard my brother's voice and saw his dirty index finger pointed at my nose.

"No you don't!" he'd say to me. "You don't stay down. You find a way to get up. You don't let anyone keep you down."

Doug was diagnosed with Alzheimer's a couple of years ago, and every time I see him, I tell him, "You don't quit, brother. You don't let this thing keep you down. You get up. You keep fighting."

He smiles his best shit-eating grin and gives me a big hug. I close my eyes extra tight to keep the tears at bay and pray for time to stand still while we embrace.

My brother's words kept me going many times throughout my military career and in civilian jobs. Without his love and inspirational talks, I doubt I would have made it through some of the toughest parts of my military training and career. Discerning when and how to fight back was not a lesson I really understood at age four. But now, after a twenty-four-year career in the Air Force and the Air National Guard, I certainly have a better grasp on when to hold my tongue and keep the peace, and when to get up and kick some ass.

"Don't give up! You keep on fighting. Don't you ever quit!"

Mary Baker works for a private consulting firm, assisting communities to find ways to be more resilient and sustainable. She is a founding member of the Nebraska Warrior Writers and a contributing author to From Warriors to Warrior Writers. *Mary presents at various veteran events and functions and is looking forward to civilian retirement and writing full time.*

Armor

Tanya Whitney, Master Sergeant, US Army, Retired
March 1983–July 2010

In 1983, I left home on a grand adventure. Flying for the first time, I traveled from New Orleans, Louisiana, to Philadelphia, Pennsylvania, to attend Army Basic Training at Fort Dix, New Jersey. This was the farthest I had ever traveled from home and my first time traveling without any family and friends. I was excited and fearful all at the same time: excited to be on this new journey, afraid of what was going to happen, and nervous about making it through training.

From Philadelphia, recruits were loaded onto a bus for Fort Dix. It was after midnight when we arrived and were told we'd be able to sleep in. At four o'clock in the morning, the drill sergeants screamed down the halls, beating on metal trash cans and waking up the whole building.

Thus began our training.

A few days after our arrival, the Army issued us uniforms. We were in line like cattle going through chutes to slaughter. We were one of the first groups to receive the Army's new battle dress uniforms (BDUs). They were so new, the olive drab, browns, and blacks were bright and crisp to our eyes. In contrast, they issued us the old, olive-drab green, field jackets.

The first time I put on my BDUs, it made me feel like somebody. I remember looking in the mirror, seeing my camo-covered reflection, and thinking, *Who is this soldier staring back at me?*

It was as though a whole different person stood there, not the shy tomboy/nobody who once existed. I never wanted to take that uniform off and revert to being a nobody ever again. Wearing the uniform, I exuded pride, holding my shoulders back and my head high. I stood tall, no longer hunching over and trying to hide.

After basic training, I was given a week's leave before going to my next duty station. Wearing my dress uniform with my single Army Service Ribbon (also known as the fruit loop ribbon) and marksman badges displayed, I strutted through the airport on my way home. Even after arriving home, I visited family and friends in uniform. In my mind, being dressed in BDUs and dress greens gave me a new identity. The uniform told the world that I was part of a small elite group, a member of the US Army.

I had completed my initial training, but I still had to complete my Advanced Individual Training before I felt I could claim the coveted title of "soldier." At home, all anyone saw was the soldier standing before them.

After my leave, I was stationed at Fort Eustis, Virginia, where I began my training as an airplane repairer. I was so happy to be on my way to becoming a fully trained soldier. Four months later, I graduated and received my qualification badge. That day, when the Aircraft Crewman Badge was pinned onto my uniform, I became a full-fledged soldier, no longer a trainee. The time had arrived when I would be assigned to a permanent duty station and begin my Army career.

The uniform became even more important to my identity as I moved through the ranks and was presented with awards. The addition of patches on my BDUs and ribbons on my dress greens showcased my achievements. I stood tall and proud. Wearing my uniform gave me strength and confidence. Each change of rank signified the trust and faith the Army had in me as a leader, encouraging me to continue. Every decoration, ribbon, and badge denoted I was willing to serve above and beyond the call of duty and made me believe in myself.

As the years passed, the rank and the uniform became my armor. Serving in the military was my sole purpose in life, at times to the detriment of my family and friends. My service took me to places around the world I had only dreamed of visiting as a child. While

I felt privileged to explore new wonders, there was a trade-off. Holidays, birthdays, weddings, and funerals were among the many things I missed while serving my country. Friendships fell by the wayside as our lives went in different directions. Friends at home didn't understand my military persona. Friends made in the Army were lost through transfers, duty assignment changes, and the end of enlistments.

Time passed to where over half my life had been spent in uniform. My first name was now Sergeant and everything in my life was camo-themed and revolved around my military service. I lived, breathed, and dreamed Army! Until the fateful day I was called in to discuss the results of my medical evaluation board (MEB).

A severe knee injury sustained during combat training was threatening to end my meaningful career at eighteen years of active-duty service. The board recommended discharge, which would force me to take off the uniform that gave me purpose. I could accept the medical discharge or retire with twenty-five years of credited service for a National Guard retirement. As I walked down the hospital hall, I believed my life was over. Outside, I sat in my car for a few moments, digesting the words of the board. I glanced at the passenger seat and saw the books for my Classical Literature class. It triggered a memory from a previous lecture about the works of Homer and I remembered our discussion of Hector and the siege of Troy.

Like Hector in Homer's epic *The Iliad*, my identity had become intertwined with my uniform. It was my shield against the world. I thought, *Who am I if I take off my armor?*

Hector was glorified by his armor. It empowered him and enabled him to strike fear into the hearts of his enemies. My uniform told the world I was a well-trained professional. Much like Hector, my highly decorated uniform demanded the respect of peers, subordinates, and even in some cases, superiors. The uniform with its medals, patches, and badges signified a warrior who served valiantly and honorably. I believed I was a different person in uniform, a warrior. I was confident and assured of my place in the Army and the world . . . until the MEB changed everything.

The MEB report highlighted the toll my military service and

deployments had taken on my body. With only two years left before being able to fully retire with an active-duty retirement, I wasn't sure I would make it. After several days of back-and-forth conversations, the MEB and my commander came to an agreement. They decided I could finish my last two years of active duty and retire with an immediate annuity rather than be medically discharged.

Two years to begin the transition to civilian life. Two years to wonder what I was going to do. I had no idea how I was going to function without the shield of my uniform. Two years to figure out how to live outside of the military. It was a difficult period in my life.

Many of my experiences were similar to Hector's experiences when he returned home after so long away. Hector frightened his son while in his helmet and armor. My kids had never known their mom out of uniform. They only knew me as a soldier. Whereas Hector's son recognized him when he removed his helmet, my family didn't recognize this latest version of Mom or know how to deal with her being around more often. Quite frankly, neither did I.

I was slowly becoming what I never wanted to be, a "secondary" person, distinguished by who their spouse was or which kids were theirs.

In the Army, I had become my own person, knowing who I was and what I was capable of doing. I didn't know who I was without my uniform on or how to act without the security of my BDUs. The uniform was my strength. Or so I believed then.

After retirement, I worked for a year and a half as a Department of the Army civilian employee, serving in the same position I held during active duty. The job was supposed to help ease the transition to the civilian world. Unfortunately, it only made things worse. I was constantly butting heads with my supervisor. He had been a civilian employee his whole career, never having served in the military. My outward identity was a reflection of my civilian status; however, my inward identity still resonated with my military service. It was a battle between the two identities. He couldn't understand how difficult the process was to go from a total of nearly twenty-eight years of wearing a military uniform to being a civilian and wearing no uniform.

One day I realized that to take control of my life and redirect my future, I had to completely reinvent myself. Trying to straddle the two worlds was like having a split personality and it was driving me crazy (crazier than normal).

I quit my civilian job with the Army and returned to my hometown. I learned my worth was not in the uniform but in the person who wore the uniform. My strength was in the person I became while wearing the uniform. The strength didn't go away when I stored those uniforms away.

I volunteered with several veterans' organizations as my way to keep a connection of brotherhood and sisterhood typically lost when leaving active-duty service. To get to know my kids better, I volunteered at their school with other band and athletic parents. I slowly became Mrs. Whitney or was seen as Robert's or Rebekah's mom. I was no longer Sergeant Whitney.

Wearing the same school colors I had worn during my high school days gave me a sense of pride. I became a coach for their cross country and track teams where I could teach the kids how to be warriors and help them become confident and responsible young adults.

Though the uniform and the warrior mode will always be a part of me, the premise upon which my life was built is now behind me. Unlike Hector who did not believe he had a life beyond his armor, I have built a new identity beyond my uniform. I have reinvented myself and found a way to have a life without my old shields in place. I have manufactured a new set of armor that I wear today. Retirement has finally become comfortable and easygoing. Years later I can look back on my military service with a melancholy smile. Those years, good or bad, have molded my character and my outlook on life and are a large part of the person I am today.

I have learned to take the personal courage and the warrior ethos of never quitting that the Army instilled in me and utilize them to rebuild my life after my military service. Life has taken on a series of new identities. Each one is a portion of who I am now. I am an Army retiree, a member of an elite group of individuals. I am a veteran of both Operation Iraqi Freedom and Enduring Freedom, recognized by my brothers and sisters for my combat service. I am a high school cross country and track and field coach, mentoring young adults. I am a volunteer in my community, assisting both civilians and veterans, willing to serve whenever and wherever I can. I am a poet and author, published within the civilian and military literary communities. I am a wife and mother.

Armor free, I am me.

After retiring, Tanya Whitney returned to Sorrento, Louisana, with her husband and two children. Since returning home, she has volunteered with several local veterans' groups serving the community. She is the head coach for the St. Amant High School Gators Cross Country team and serves as an assistant track and field coach for St. Amant High.

Learning the Ropes

Reinetta Vaneendenburg, Captain, USN, Retired
August 1979–September 2016

"A rum and Coke, please," the ensign said to the muscled bartender, placing her brand-new dress hat, its glaring white crown still in pristine condition, tentatively on the sticky bar. With only a five in her wallet, she had enough for one drink—a reward for making it through her first week at a Navy aviation squadron.

"You might want to remove that," nodded the wizened warrant officer in faded flight coveralls; the guys at the squadron called them pickle suits.

"Excuse me?" she said as the bartender placed the highball in front of her. She pulled her white, flared skirt down and checked to ensure the straightness of her gig line—the line formed by the shirt front edge to the belt buckle—which had become more of habit than necessity.

The warrant officer reached over the oval-shaped hat for a handful of pretzels from a harvest-green, plastic bowl.

The garage-sized officers' bar on Naval Air Station North Island was replete with shield-shaped plaques and ball caps from fliers across the globe. It smelled of sweat and heartbreak. The crowded area's smoky haziness was in stark relief to the pearly Coronado Friday afternoon.

"There's plenty of room," she said.

He shrugged, lighting a Marlboro. "Just trying to save you some dough."

The oversized brass bell that hung by the door shrieked, then shrieked again, parting the chatter of the men.

"What's that?" she asked. "What happened? Why is everyone looking at me?"

"Drinks on the girl!" shouted a pickle-suited guy at the bell, pointing directly at her.

She glared at the grinning warrant officer, wondering how to pay for the men's drinks this far from payday.

National Endowment for the Arts Military Veteran Fellow Reinetta Van is a regular contributor to The War Horse. *The essay collection* Navy Blues: Between WAVES and Warriors *is under consideration for publishing. The oral history* US Navy Women Line Officers: From Support to Spear Tip *is under contract. The limited-edition* Armed Forces Staff College Fifty-Year Commemorative History *was published in 1996.*

Are You Willing to Pay the Price?

Beverly (Christie) Smith, Staff Sergeant, USAF, Retired
October 1976–October 1996

In 1976, I was twenty years old, working in a convenience store, making minimum wage, and going nowhere. I couldn't afford to go to college and had no skills. I had known several people in the military making a decent living, so I decided to check out my options. I chose the Air Force because I didn't like the Navy uniforms. I had already ruled out the Army and Marines as too rough. The military would feed me, clothe me, house me, train me, and pay me. Wow!

The only downside was that I would have to leave my mom. Man, that hurt. It took me five times before I finally made it up that plane ramp when I was leaving for basic training.

There was a test program allowing women to perform security police duties, including guarding airplanes and nuclear missiles.

At that time, I thought our country was very progressive. After all, it was 1976. We didn't give a thought to the fact that we were breaking all types of barriers.

After basic training at Lackland Air Force Base, Texas, there were one hundred women in the initial security police training flights. We all graduated from the classroom training and progressed to the Air Base Ground Defense physical training, which included firing weapons, defending ground areas, forward movements, etc. We were so young and naïve. We didn't realize not all military personnel accepted women going into the security police (SP) field. The first openly hostile military person I encountered was an instructor teaching us how to fire the M60 machine gun.

Most male SPs have the upper body strength to hold the 28.6-pound weapon at arm level and jack a round into the chamber. Women (most of us less than 125 pounds) didn't have the strength to handle that task, so we pressed the end of the weapon on our thigh to accomplish the job. Our instructor failed us and wouldn't let us progress with training because we didn't hold the weapon correctly.

The commander was notified of the situation and marched down the hill. I can still see him in my mind's eye. The instructor told him what was going on, and the commander asked me to show him how I performed the task. I did.

He found a male trainee similar in size and had him perform the task. That man did it the same way I did.

The commander was furious at the instructor. "Don't you ever have me come down here for something like this again! These women accomplished the task."

A total of seventy-five women successfully graduated from the course.

I was in awe that the commander stood up for us, and it changed my life. At the time, I just pressed forward with the tasks, but later, his defense was always in the back of my mind, reminding me that if I was bullied, I could speak out and not let people run over me.

Women were only allowed to go to four bases as part of the test program: Osan, Republic of Korea; Nellis, Nevada; Barksdale, Louisiana; and Grand Forks, North Dakota. I chose Osan, because it was my chance to see another country.

In February 1977, three women arrived in Osan for our first assignment. We were so excited. I was put on the mid-shift (ten at night until seven in the morning, six days a week). At one point, I was working inside a controlled area behind concertina wire, guarding nuclear weapons. During this shift, my sergeant told me to sweep and mop the inside area. No one else had ever performed this task.

I explained to my sergeant that this wasn't a regular task. Just because I was a girl didn't mean I should do that job. He said to do it anyway.

"No, I won't do it."

He said he would give me a letter of reprimand if I didn't complete the task. I said I understood.

The next shift, the lieutenant in charge called me in and asked me to explain. I gave him the information. He asked me to complete the task—again, I refused. I repeated the argument that just because I was a woman didn't mean I should be singled out for that task.

I received a letter of reprimand.

The important thing was that I stood up for myself and the women who would come after me. I knowingly paid the price for my action, because I felt it was important. It went against my code of being bullied, and I wasn't going to accept it. I also wanted the men to know that I was a security policewoman—not housekeeping.

I wanted to have a child. While still in Korea, I got pregnant. My commander called me and my boyfriend (now husband of forty-four years and the love of my life) into his office. He asked when we were getting married. We said that we weren't.

He couldn't understand our decision. Again, I stood up for myself and what I wanted. Not an easy task when facing your commander.

In 1979, our test program was terminated by Congress. The country just wasn't ready for women to be in combat roles. Our country wasn't as progressive as I thought. (The AF reintroduced women into the security police in 1985 where they are still serving and succeeding. The initial seventy-five women made not only AF history, but we were the first women to ever serve in a combat role.)

After our test program was terminated, I chose to go into the contracting/purchasing field. Over the next eighteen years of service, the lessons I learned while with the security police were always in the back of my mind. I used them in my life anytime I had to stand up for myself.

When I was the administrator for the food service contract for Lackland AFB in San Antonio, Texas, the contractor filed a lawsuit against the AF because I refused to give him all of the monies he requested for an annual labor increase. I could justify some of the funds requested but not all of what he was used to receiving.

Long story short, the female contracting officer and I were strongly encouraged by our commander to give the contractor whatever he wanted. We stood firm in our decision. As a result, we received very low appraisals and terrible job assignments, but it was worth it to do what was right. It took seven years before we were vindicated. The contractor lost all future contracts with the military due to the issues discovered during the lawsuit.

Hear me on this: standing up for yourself (and others) isn't for sissies. There are always pros and cons to your decision. Sometimes there's a price to pay.

Get to know yourself and decide what you feel is important enough to stand up for. Future generations are counting on you.

If You're Going to Be Tough . . .

Taryn Pike, Sergeant, US Army National Guard
February 2002–February 2014

I have boys. Wylie is six and Weston is four, and they are officially in the wrestling stage of their lives. Every stick-like object is a sword, and every obstacle mere inches above ground level is solely there to be climbed. Life is loud, boisterous, full of scraped knees, and fun, my friend.

I started off overcautious as every other first-time mom, but as life with kids will have it, I threw in the proverbial towel by kid two. Second-borns, am I right? The point where moms stop sanitizing car seats and resort to shouting, "Hey! Are you guys okay?" when there's no visual.

I'm swimming deep in this stage of life, and some days, I'm barely keeping my head above water. But last year I committed to genuinely reflect and process past experiences that aren't so pleasant. Again, as life will have it, this process has me exploring a literal (as in words) moment in motherhood.

A wise mother once said, "If you're gonna be rough, you better be tough."

(That's me by the way; I'm the wise mother.)

I quickly tired of the tattling and adopted this response in lieu of justice. Not sure if I adopted this sentiment from my own mother, but I suspect she maintained her own version through the years.

Wylie smashed your Lego gun when you were shooting him off the couch?

Sorry, bud. If you're going to be rough, you better be tough.

Wrestling with Weston and bonked your head into the wall?

Well, sorry, dude. But, if you're going to be rough, you better be tough.

See where I'm going here? It's versatile, all-encompassing, sympathetic yet deflective. It's genius. Yet, every time I deploy my wise old adage, a part of me pauses. Have I said this before? Have I heard this before?

Why does this feel weird?

It took me a few months to recognize the connection, but I realize I've been telling myself some version of this for years. Some version that feels dismissive. That feels like I'm excusing bad behavior for the sake of convenience. The deeper I dive, the more certain I am that this phrase, and versions of it, have been my mechanism to excuse, diminish, and accept events or behaviors that were uncomfortable since I was sixteen years old. Let's begin there.

In 2002, my parents and I signed my Army enlistment papers together. It was a week after my seventeenth birthday and four short months after 9/11. When people asked why I joined, I replied with the obligatory "patriotic calling."

Truth was, my service wasn't so much a deep-felt calling as it was an opportunity to flee my tiny Midwest hometown where I had just been sexually assaulted by my mother's adopted brother.

I didn't know how to navigate the fallout after that assault, and it's fair to say my mother didn't either. I was never encouraged to report him, and although I understand (even appreciate at times) my family's hesitation to publicize that information, as a young woman, I felt like it was "swept under the rug." I didn't understand the impact that experience would have on my life, but I understood that reporting my uncle would be complicated. Instead of processing that experience, I accepted that he "was just drunk" and "he didn't mean it" and to just "stay away from him." And there it is. Just like that, my coping mechanism was off to the races.

At seventeen and just a few days after the end of my junior year in high school, I left for basic training. I would complete basic training over the summer, return home to finish high school, and leave again after graduation to complete advanced training. I was in an engineering unit; there were eight females in our company of 200+ males. And we eight were the center of attention. We were the butt of every joke, the examples whether we excelled or failed, the body of every man's attention, good or bad.

Don't misunderstand this claim; I was in basic training with a forty-four-year-old ex-body builder from New York, two other stout farm girls from the Dakotas, and a handful of other women, all beautiful in their own right, but when you're dripping in sweat, no makeup, hair tied up in a bun, etc., we likely wouldn't have garnered a second look in the civilian world. Yet here we were. The object of affection or resentment or both, no matter what we did. It was the beginning of a decade-long stint of not knowing how the hell to act and facing relentless criticism no matter the choice.

I told myself, "You joined the Army. What did you expect?"

And I soldiered on.

I was legitimately shocked when a fellow female trainee told me she was sleeping with one of the drill sergeants.

"What?!"

She replied, "Most of the girls in our company are."

When a drill sergeant came and got me in the middle of the night during week six, I wasn't surprised. What did I expect? (For the record, and not that it matters, I wriggled my way out of that encounter unscathed.)

I told myself, "You joined the Army. What did you expect?"

And I soldiered on.

My first time in Afghanistan, as a bright nineteen-year-old E-4, I was put in a position where the next enlisted counterpart was an E-9, and the rest were commissioned officers. An E-4 can be considered entry-level, while E-9 and commissioned officers equate to upper management. The position was arranging all flight support for personnel or equipment across Army Aviation, Air Force, and Marines/Navy. I killed that job. I understood it, I improved the process, and I became the "go-to" for my counterparts for training or help. I was immensely proud of my work, and the gentlemen I worked with day-to-day treated me with respect.

Unfortunately, the more respect I gained from that specific group, the more criticism I faced from others.

Women in the military and civilian workplaces are all too often accused of seducing their way to the top or some other ridiculous notion. God forbid we could just be good at our jobs.

As a kid, I was always an overachiever. I was class president from eighth grade to senior year, student council vice president, homecoming royalty, honor graduate; worked twenty-plus hours a week as a waitress; and was voted most musical, most crazy, Miss Congeniality, and more. No joke; I did it all while being kind, friendly, and outgoing.

At nineteen years old in Afghanistan, I adapted my otherwise enthusiastic and likable personality. I thought I could squash the claims that my success was just some trick or coercion on my part by being just as assertive, confident, and brash as the boys. In other words, I became an asshole to play the game.

I told myself, "If you can't run with the big dogs, stay on the porch."

And I soldiered on.

A little over a year after I returned home from that first deployment, I retrained as a military police officer and volunteered for another deployment to Afghanistan. My last duty rotation in-country was on a small forward operating base. A few weeks before going home, I was sexually assaulted by my battalion command sergeant major (many ranks above me in the command structure).

Because I was part of a seven-man detachment, the only female, and the only military police, I didn't report it past my squad leader. I was too afraid of being held back in-country and not getting home. I imagine the command sergeant major knew I wouldn't bring anything forward, and he made it a point to seek me out for the next few weeks to introduce me to other high-ranking individuals. I knew by his behavior these other men knew what happened and knew I couldn't do a damn thing about it. I'm still not sure what his unspoken message was, but I suspected, had I been there longer, I would've been assaulted by these other men. It was one of the most humiliating and degrading times in my life.

But I told myself, "Boys will be boys, right?"

And I soldiered on.

I was home for two years after that deployment. I returned to my original engineering unit, finished college, and applied for pilot school with the Army Aviation unit. Pilot selection is tough; you must test academically and athletically and then be selected by a panel of pilots and officers. By this point, I was an impressive young soldier on paper and was selected to fill one of the pilot slots. Weeks later, I got orders to deploy with my current unit, and I had the choice to attend pilot school or go back to Afghanistan.

Seems like an easy choice, right? Problem was that my little brother was in my engineering unit and was deploying no matter what. This would be my third twelve-plus month tour to Afghanistan in a span of six years, and I was hesitant to go. But I didn't want to miss the opportunity to serve with my brother, and the Aviation unit said they would hold my pilot slot until I got back. I was his big sister with two tours under my belt, and I believed I could support him; we'd undergo this experience together.

I also knew how lonely it was, both over there and coming home, not having family who understood that readjustment period. I was glad we'd have each other to lean on.

I distinctly remember going to my last pre-deployment health screening, and the mental health officer offered me an out. He asked if I was sure I was ready to deploy again; it seemed to him like too many deployments too fast.

Nah, I'm good.

I told myself, after all, I signed up for this.

And I soldiered on.

This last tour in Afghanistan was particularly hard. My brother, raised with four sisters, is kind and respectful and doesn't play into the big-boy bravado behavior. Unfortunately, our fellow soldiers did, and when they weren't persecuting him for walking with me to the chow hall or gym tent, they were whispering crude remarks meant for us to hear.

The bullshit I dismissed, but my brother couldn't. I can't equate that deployment environment to anything civilian side. If you know, you know. If you haven't been there, it's hard to explain. Every move you make is watched by men: walking to the bathroom, going for a run, eating at the chow hall, doing your work. They loathe you, harass you, demean you, sexualize you, diminish you, etc. Their behavior and response toward women make or break your experience. And this time, it broke mine.

There was a moment I shifted. We had just come off a mission and hadn't slept for about twenty hours. We got to the motor pool, put up our equipment, and headed to our tents to shower and sleep. My brother and I were walking to my hut, and my nemesis squad leader stopped us. He told my brother he wasn't going to sleep but had to report to a twelve-hour guard shift.

"Why?" It was the natural question.

"Ask your sister." This man loved to punish my brother to hurt me, and this time, I toppled down the back side of my tipping point. I was so livid with anger in the moment, I could only cry and apologize to my brother. I lost all resolve, and it was the beginning of the end.

All these experiences—the men I fought beside being cruel or disgusting or dismissive or degrading—finally caught up with me. Having my brother there to bear witness proved too much. I felt ashamed and guilty for what he heard, saw, and endured on my behalf. We were stuck in a relentless cycle of feeling bad for each other.

I was filled with a palpable resentment and hatred for these men, and it manifested to a full-on mental breakdown. I was riddled with anxiety to the point where I was involuntarily shaking almost all day. I barely spoke to people without crying, and I clung to my brother's side. I was dependent on him to get me through daily tasks.

Every day all day, I walked around with a loaded M14 on my back, willing myself to live. I just had to survive until my mid-tour leave where my brother and I would go home for two weeks. I knew I wasn't going to return to Afghanistan from leave, and I desperately didn't want my brother to escort my dead body home before then.

I was resolved to either go AWOL (absent without leave) and be arrested or kill myself after I saw my parents and sisters. I had no emotion attached to those options. If you've ever been in the deep, dark, depression pit of hell where suicide is comforting, you understand that lack of feeling.

About a week before my brother and I left for leave, I walked to the USO tent, stood in line for the phones, and called an old sergeant major from my first tour. I didn't say a word when he answered the phone; I just started sobbing. He patiently waited for me to gather myself and tell him I couldn't be there anymore. He arranged for a mental health officer to meet me in the States, and I vaguely remember signing an affidavit (that I didn't write) stating I was "unfit for duty." A male NCO was assigned to escort me to Fort Dix, New Jersey, where I would be out-processed. This NCO never left my side, even through the medical and mental evaluations. If I wasn't already so sad, it would've been sad.

After ten years and three combat tours, I claimed (out loud, mind you) that I didn't feel well mentally. I was immediately separated from the Army. Fort Dix was the last contact I had with Army personnel. I explicitly told the Army I was suicidal, and they pushed me out the door with a wave and a good luck. When I say I struggled, I mean I struggled.

I tried to resume a "normal" life, but I battled with suicidal thoughts daily and needed safeguards in place. I found a counselor at the Veterans' Center, which is an independent organization not associated with Veterans Affairs or any branch of service, and moved into a studio apartment nearby so I could check in with her every day. I didn't trust myself to keep living, let alone function in the real world. I crawled and scraped my way out of that hole for years.

While I stayed home and separated from the military, my brother returned to Afghanistan for the next four months to finish that deployment. His experience after I left the unit was completely different in a positive way. That may be the only saving grace about my leaving. I still feel guilt and shame for the hardship he sustained because of me.

At my brother's homecoming ceremony, nobody spoke to me. I served with some of those men for years during multiple tours, and I considered them friends and brothers-in-arms. I was invisible to them and realized I had nothing to show for my ten years of service. I never got to attend pilot school; I'll never receive retirement benefits; and I lost nearly every friend I had through my early adulthood years. I had effectively thrown away my life as I knew it, all to save it.

Up to that point, I had given my life to my military career, excelling in leadership schools and volunteering for any mission I could. This year marks ten years since I left the Army yet would have been my retirement had I stayed in. To stay alive and regain my mental health, I gave up the service I loved and dedicated ten years of my life to. That sacrifice, one of many servicemembers bear, is never lost on me.

Being ignored was devastating, but I had to move on as a civilian, and I told myself, "Out of sight, out of mind."

It took nearly ten years after leaving the military to actually reflect on my time served objectively. Ten years of dragging myself out of some incredibly dark and depressive states. Ten years of avoiding anything or anyone who reminded me of my time in service. Ten years to reach the point of acknowledging my service for the good it was, grieving the loss of a career I wanted, and giving myself grace for choosing my mental health.

A few years ago, my brother graduated from Officer Candidate School and had a pinning ceremony for his lieutenant bar. He chose me to give him his first salute as an officer. For the first time in seven years, I was in the same room with him and other men in uniform, some whom I served with. It's strange what the mind and heart react to, and the thought of saluting him brought on guilt and shame. I didn't feel like I deserved to salute anymore. It felt like I sacrificed the right to salute when I separated. Of course, I didn't tell him that. I was just deeply honored he chose me. Through tears and a shaking hand, I gave my little brother his first salute as an officer and then snuck in a hug, which was not customary. He chuckled. That one moment was so healing for me, and I hope for him as well.

We don't talk about that deployment much. I think it's equally painful for both of us, and some things don't need to be said. We talk about his career now. He's a leader, and I'm proud of the example he sets and the expectations he holds for how his soldiers conduct themselves.

The world needs more men like him: men who value colleagues and subordinates solely on ability and attitude and consciously make efforts to set aside presumptions. We're humans, and as humans, we have prejudices whether we acknowledge them or not. The challenge is recognizing them and making the right decision regardless. My brother is a "no excuse for bad behavior" kind of guy, and I'm just over here taking notes.

Feminist Andrea Dworkin wrote, "Woman is not born: she is made. In the making, her humanity is destroyed. She becomes symbol of this, symbol of that: mother of the earth, slut of the universe; but she never becomes herself because it is forbidden for her to do so."

From day one in basic training, we women were objects, symbols for someone else. In my formative years of womanhood, kindness was sexualized, and assuredness was demonized. I acclimated to a world of harsh stereotypes and tried desperately to play the game and appease everyone. For the record, that doesn't work. Every time I dismissed that gut feeling and brushed bad things under the rug, I gave up a little chunk of myself.

It's important to recognize the stories we tell ourselves. Recognize the excuses we make for others and ourselves. Left unchecked, our "self" gets dangerously lost in lies. There were so many points in my life and career where I could've done things differently. I didn't deserve to be treated badly just because I was there. Because I was a female.

Instead of the lies I told along the way, I could have told myself, "Hey, girl, you actually don't have to be rough to be tough." I could have shifted the trajectory of my life.

That's the silver lining though—you can shift.

Maybe it's old age or motherhood or just enough tough life lessons that have allowed me to deeply root myself into a belief system. My moral compass now doesn't give wiggle room for excuses, and I am well aware of how I expect to be treated by others and how I treat others in return.

Can you just imagine if young women had unshakable standards from the get-go? Or, as in true boy-mom fashion, if young men had unshakable standards from the get-go? This brings me back to my wise old adage of being tough and rough and blah, blah, blah.

Maybe you don't have to be tough. Maybe introducing these seemingly harmless phrases will crack open the door to risky interpretation.

Years ago, I read this quote from Margaret Atwood, "Men are afraid that women will laugh at them. Women are afraid that men will kill them."

I cannot unhear it. It's relevant, true, hard to stomach and, for years, was my mantra toward the opposite sex. I used this phrase to make sense of things men did, and it unintentionally let them off the hook. They're villains, don't you know? If I only expected bad behavior, I was never disappointed.

Well . . .

Karma, The Universe, God, or whatever you believe had a thing (actually, two) to say about that. The moment I delivered each of my bouncing boys into this world was pure magic and terror all in one. The responsibility of raising men has me straddling the feminist line and challenging my beliefs about how men show up. I am charged with teaching my men to find their value in this world as well as the value of the women they share it with. That responsibility leaves little room for the comfortable excuses I had settled into.

Now, I'm not sure that I'll hang up my "rough to be tough" saying altogether with the boys. I mean, they are constantly climbing things, and there are days I need a fallback, but I'm more careful now. I know words are heavy with meaning and deserve to be examined.

So, Sister, be sure the words you use serve you and align with your unshakable standards in life. Let them be words that demonstrate strength and compassion and whole-hearted resilience for goodness in this world. Words can change everything.

Taryn Pike resides in the Black Hills of South Dakota with her husband and two sons. She works as a real estate advisor, contract land agent, and investor in both Texas and South Dakota. In her downtime, she enjoys camping, hiking, woodworking, writing, and spending time with her large and loud family.

The Uphill Climb Is Worth It!

Dr. Cherryann Joseph, Colonel, US Army, Retired
December 1988–February 2022

"You're under investigation."

Dreaded words no military leader ever wants to hear. Anxiety bowled me over as I listened to the investigating officer's (IO) words. After the meeting, I reflected on how I got into this mess. Perhaps I could have avoided it if I hadn't ignored certain common-sense leadership practices. Leadership expert John C. Maxwell's advice that "everything worthwhile is uphill" deeply resonated with me. I buckled up for an arduous climb that would test my resolve and faith.

I had an inkling something was wrong. Several weeks earlier, I clicked on my Army personnel record while showing a non-commissioned officer how to use a data system. An unexpected "flag" popped up. I switched screens to avoid further humiliation. This administrative flag meant I couldn't travel or get any favorable actions, including passes, awards, and promotions.

What did I do to merit the first flag of my decades-long career? I had a squeaky-clean reputation and an unblemished record. No one would call me a superstar, but my talent and efforts earned me the rank of lieutenant colonel. My supervisor, who was also the unit's chief of staff, didn't bother counseling me before placing the flag. Thus, I entered unfamiliar territory as the unwitting subject of not one but two investigations.

Something was not right—a premonition that helped me remain

calm during the meeting as the IO said, "You're accused of two cases of bullying and one case of sexual harassment."

After rebutting these allegations, I hurried back to my office and shut the door. Overwhelmed by fear and anxiety, I thought about the possible negative impacts on my career. A promotion board had recently reviewed my records for promotion to colonel. A guilty verdict meant no promotion and a swift end to my military career. I leaned heavily on my faith as I prayed for wisdom on how to navigate through this dark valley.

My two male accusers were both Army Active Guard Reserve (AGR) majors. The only good thing I saw from the whole scenario was I couldn't be called a racist because one was Black and the other White. The Black major served on my Training and Operations staff while the White one supervised the Human Resources (HR) section. Not long after meeting them, I learned both had a history of filing complaints and dodging responsibilities.

Without question, this incident was the lowest point in my time with the rear detachment of this Army Reserve one-star command. Similar to previous assignments, I tried to add value and help co-workers succeed. Before the pandemic, I set up a monthly speaker series and used it to feature the unit's high-performing NCOs and junior officers. Both soldiers and civilians seemed to enjoy the series, which helped us build unit camaraderie while growing professionally. I also regularly treated my team to lunch or bought them breakfast. It surprised me to hear anyone thought I bullied or sexually harassed them.

This midwestern, US-based detachment had operated for almost a month when I came on board as the Training and Operations Officer in Charge (OIC). I was one of four female officers in a unit with less than 10 percent of soldiers from minority backgrounds. Most of the soldiers were reservists organic to the unit, a handful were AGR members (full-timers), and the rest were volunteers like me.

My soldiers were used to doing things their way, and some were not receptive to an outsider—especially one from New York—holding them accountable. Nevertheless, I strove to build rapport and get to know them better. I put together a leader book with their career expectations, goals, families, hobbies, and other things leaders ought to know about their soldiers. I also met with each of them individually to learn more about them.

My relationship with my boss wasn't a good one. He told me he was going to do everything in his power to get me fired. He claimed I made him look stupid in front of the commander.

During a counseling session, he tried to coerce me into agreeing with his assessment of my leadership. I fervently disagreed with his assessment because it was based on falsehoods and complaints from the HR OIC and his wife. I pleaded with him to speak to other people to validate these claims. Convinced of my toxic leadership, he refused to get feedback from anyone else.

We went back and forth for almost three hours; he called me a toxic leader while I accused him of being biased and unfair. I asked to meet with the commander.

With my boss in attendance, I disclosed several instances when he undermined my authority and dumped his duties on me. He furiously disputed these claims and then inadvertently confirmed them. After almost six months on the job, he revealed he didn't know the commander's philosophy, strategy, and priorities.

The commander corrected him for misquoting me several times as my boss tried to portray me as an angry Black woman.

I repeated my frustrations with the work environment and carelessly blurted out, "I want to resign."

"If that is what you really want, I won't stand in your way," the commander said.

Disappointed by his reply, I didn't respond.

He continued, "Think it over and let me know what you decide after the Christmas break."

I agreed and left his office in a state of anxiety.

After the holiday, I returned to the unit and shared the situation with two senior civilians. They told me I was making a big difference and helping to accomplish the mission. They begged me not to leave. After praying and reflecting on my options, I decided to stay and continue fighting the uphill battle to clear my name.

Shortly after my decision to remain, I found out about the accusations against me.

I reflected on my interactions with the two complainants. The Black officer accused me of bullying and sexual harassment. Despite complaints about his work habits, I gave him a chance to prove himself as the inspection program OIC. Three months before the case against me, we went on a temporary duty trip. It was the first inspection of the year, so I tagged along to observe and mentor him. To my surprise, he kept delaying planning his travel arrangements and appeased me with remarks such as, "Don't worry, ma'am, I'll get it done."

About a week before the travel date, I received an email notification that his government travel card was suspended.

He awkwardly admitted, "I have a balance over ninety days late. I'm not sure how I can travel."

I came up with a plan for him to travel using alternative funding. "I will get the rental car and give you a ride to and from the hotel and duty location."

In my attempt to help him, I forgot the wise leadership practice of avoiding meeting or traveling alone with lower-ranking soldiers, especially those of the opposite sex.

When we arrived at the airport, I found out he had reserved a rental car. Despite my irritation, I canceled my rental. "Let's not waste travel funds with two rental cars."

He was visibly upset. As we drove, I learned he wanted to visit his mother whom he hadn't seen in almost two years. I reluctantly said, "Let me get some items from Walmart, then you can drop me off at the hotel. You can use the car for what you need."

His wife called while I was in the store. From his demeanor when I returned, it was clear they had a tense exchange.

I asked, "Would she have a problem with a female being in the car with you?"

He mumbled, "Yes, ma'am."

"Did you tell her who is in the car with you?"

He didn't respond. After he dropped me off, I decided to find another way to get to the duty location.

To my amazement, this officer used this incident and the battle book information I collected on him as the basis of his accusations.

The second accusation came from the human resources officer.

During several mission-related exchanges, I tasked his section with planning and coordinating an administrative training workshop. He dug in his heels, asserting it wasn't his job, while aggravating me with several delaying tactics. I raised the issue to my boss, the chief of staff, who responded by saying, "Well, your section should do it."

I felt caving in would further undermine my tasking authority, so I fortified my position and kept trying to force the OIC to do the task. I now realized that instead of doubling down, I could have tried a more personable approach to resolve this impasse.

Another interaction with the HR OIC probably caused him some public embarrassment. During a briefing with the commander, I pointed out that our lodging funds were extremely low. We were only three months into the fiscal year and had spent 90 percent of our annual budget.

To me, the finance officer offered the standard, "We're working on resolving the problem, ma'am."

"I need more than that. What happened?" the commander asked.

"Higher headquarters made a mistake when they gave us funds. They told me to submit a form to request the rest of it," the human resources officer blurted out. "I'm not going to do it. It was their mistake. It's not my job to fix it!"

Using slightly colorful language, the commander told him to comply with the higher headquarters order.

In hindsight, I probably should have pulled the HR OIC aside to clarify that I didn't mean to embarrass him.

For almost three months, I was in a holding pattern while awaiting the outcomes of the two investigations. I considered my options and sought advice from colleagues and friends.

While waiting, I sank into a depressing abyss and wasn't sure how or if I could climb out. I relied on a trusted inner circle of friends and confidants who urged me to continue climbing uphill. A close friend and fellow officer counseled me to wait it out and trust God to walk me through this dark valley. Another friend and senior NCO told me to just voluntarily leave; I was tempted to take her advice.

Resigning would temporarily relieve the pressure but would not spare me from negative outcomes. Leaving would give my accusers an unearned victory while damaging my career and reputation.

It seemed like a class-action complaint swung into full motion as two investigators interrogated me. The first IO recited the bullying accusations and shared that "every witness agreed with these allegations."

The sexual harassment IO interviewed me and several witnesses. Fortunately, I had saved emails exchanged with the Black major about the travel complications. I gave those emails to the IO along with documents from my predecessors showing a pattern of misconduct by this officer. After meeting with the two IOs, I began the long wait for the results that would determine my fate.

After about three months, the results finally came in. The sexual harassment IO declared, "Based on email traffic, witness testimonies, and other documents, the claims of the accuser are not substantiated."

In his report, the second IO revealed that he discredited the testimonies of the HR OIC and his wife. He was getting ready to wrap up the case when he accidentally ran into my boss.

He asked, "How's the investigation going? Did everyone agree with me about her toxic leadership and all the accusations?"

Perplexed by this conversation, the IO decided to interview people beyond the list of names the chief gave him. He spoke to the supply OIC and civilian operations officer, who both disputed the bullying claims and gave feedback supporting my version of events and the chief's conduct. He then interviewed an NCO whom the HR OIC's wife accused me of publicly humiliating.

Baffled, the soldier said, "She always treated me with the same respect as any staff officer even though I'm only an E-5."

This sergeant's response lifted my spirits because it validated my practice of valuing people no matter their rank or position.

Those interviews validated the IO's expansion of the witness list and spun the results in my favor. His final report revealed several ways in which the chief also undermined brigade commanders and other leaders. As a result, the chief had to submit a written rebuttal to those claims. Absolved of all the charges against me, I breathed a huge sigh of relief because I finally finished this anxiety-laden uphill climb.

In the aftermath of the investigations, I refused to let my emotions hinder my ability to act according to my values. I tried to clear the air with my accusers and my boss. COVID restrictions stopped me from meeting the accusers face-to-face. I wrote them letters instead, offering sincere apologies for any harm I caused. Unsurprisingly, neither officer responded to my letter.

I dropped a letter on my boss's desk on the last day of the mission. I left the building and started my long drive home with gratitude to God for lifting me out of the dark valley by helping me overcome these accusations. A worthwhile climb that ended with my promotion to colonel, a rank I never imagined achieving when I first became an Army officer.

As John C. Maxwell says, "Failure should be our teacher, not our undertaker."

Learning from failures and adversities is an integral part of leadership. Reflecting on the entire situation, I noted several ways I could improve my leadership, interpersonal, and communication skills. Failures and mistakes are necessary elements of human experience. I encourage leaders, both young and old, to not give up when adversity strikes. Stick to your principles, lean on your faith, rely on your inner circle, learn from your mistakes, and continue climbing toward greatness, because the uphill climb is worth it!

Cherryann Joseph has a robust commitment to servant leadership. She has over three decades of military service and twelve years of teaching public school science. As a John Maxwell-certified coach, she helps people and organizations grow capacity and up-level performance.

The Invisible War

Terri Post, Private, US Army
November 1987–January 1989

* This story contains references to sexual assualt.

In 2013, I saw *The Invisible War*, a documentary about military sexual trauma. The memories came flooding back, and I didn't leave my house for three weeks. I always thought I was broken. I never knew what was wrong because I had blocked out the trauma.

I joined the Army at eighteen. My grandfather served in the Navy during World War II. After that he became a police officer and retired as a lieutenant. He was the kindest, most honorable man I knew. My admiration of him influenced my decision to become a military police officer.

At the time I enlisted, I had no prospects for college; I wasn't a very good student. Joining the military was to give me a job, teach me discipline, and open opportunities I couldn't get anywhere else.

I arrived at Ft. McClellan in Anniston, Alabama, as a wide-eyed, young woman, full of hopes and dreams of starting a new career in the service. Having spent most of my life in Maine, Alabama was a bit of a culture shock. Everything was new. There were plants I had never seen before, animals that would never survive the harsh winters I was used to, and food I had never tasted before but was ordered to eat. This was a whole new world in many ways, and I was eager to start this new adventure.

I arrived at the reception station and received my military-issued uniforms and equipment—everything needed to survive life in the Army. The next step was taking a bus to the other side of the base for basic training.

I was one of the first to arrive at my training company and was met by Drill Sergeant Lessard. He could look at your social security number and tell you where you were born. Lessard glanced over my paperwork and knew I was from Maine. "Your name is Moose. When I say 'Moose,' you say, 'Yes, Drill Sergeant.' Do you understand me, Moose?"

Still in shock and carrying more weight in my duffle bag than I weighed myself, I snapped to attention. "Yes, Drill Sergeant!"

Over the next few days, the company filled up and training began. I learned how to do things the Army way. I was taught everything from folding my clothes to polishing the brass on my uniforms. They even taught me how much to swing my arms as I marched by singing, "Nine to the front and six to the rear, that's the way we do it here."

After nine weeks of training on every topic from marching to marksmanship, I had learned how to do everything in a military manner. Armed with this rudimentary knowledge, I graduated basic combat training and moved to my chosen job training—military police (MP).

There I learned about the Uniform Code of Military Justice (UCMJ) and practiced different scenarios and how to respond to calls. Perhaps the best lesson I learned was how to diffuse a volatile situation. The easiest way to take someone into custody, after all, is for them to come with you voluntarily.

I had been at Ft. McClellan for four and a half months. Physically, I was in the best shape I'd ever been in. Mentally, I was prepared for any challenge. My parents came for graduation day. They hadn't fully supported my decision to join the military, and my relationship with my father was strained at best. That day, however, was the first time I can remember him saying he was proud of me. His words were important but difficult to believe due to our history. Never would I have imagined that he would drive from Maine to Alabama to see me graduate from Military Police School.

After graduation, we were permitted to spend time with our families. I took my parents to the post exchange where my father purchased a hat stitched with "Military Police" and the crossed pistols worn by MPs. I couldn't believe that he would spend money on anything to show how proud I had made him. It's been almost thirty-five years, and he still has that damned hat!

My parents went home, and I was on my way to Germany. I felt a sense of pride and confidence in my ability to do my job well. I had no idea that my life would change forever.

I had been at my unit for about two months and was at a party in the room next door. I had too much to drink, so I decided to go to bed. One of the sergeants made sure I made it back to my rack. I got ready for bed and quickly fell asleep. About an hour later, I woke up to that same sergeant assaulting me. The details aren't as important as the aftermath of the trauma.

After he left, I huddled in my room and waited anxiously for the platoon sergeant to arrive for work. My room was halfway down the hall from his office. After asking to speak to him privately, I reported my attack in great detail. I told him who the perpetrator was and what he had done. I informed him how I had been forced to commit acts against my will.

His response was to raise his hands above his head and say, "The guys have to blow off steam somehow."

Then he got up and left the office.

I was stunned! I was an MP, as were my assailant and the person to whom I was reporting the incident. Nothing was done. What was I supposed to do? Where could I go? Military personnel can't leave their jobs or go back home when something like that happens. I was in a foreign country, nineteen years old, and the people who were supposed to "have my six" were the very ones who perpetrated and perpetuated my trauma.

Retaliation is always a concern with military sexual trauma (MST) incidents, and my case was no exception. My attacker returned to tell me that I needed to learn to "keep my f***ing mouth shut!"

I didn't report that rape. What was the use?

Three months later, I was sexually assaulted in the barracks by another MP in my platoon . . . I didn't report that attack either.

Over the next couple of months, I self-medicated with alcohol. Eventually alcohol stopped working, so I turned to other substances. I just wanted to feel numb. I got in trouble for failing job performance. I was busted when the Army Criminal Investigation Division (CID) came through the barracks with K-9s, and I was brought up on charges for drug paraphernalia. The worse part was it was found in my roommate's wall locker, but she had moved back to the States months earlier. My commanding officer gave me the option of a court-marshal or an Article 15 to be "chaptered out."

I chose the Article 15, received forty-five days extra duty and restriction, loss of rank and lost one third of my pay for two months. I had to be escorted to the chow hall, usually by one or both men who violated me. To top it all off, I watched both get promoted while I was waiting to get kicked out of the Army.

I joined the Army in 1988 . . . long before Tailhook and Vanessa Guillen. There was no Sexual Harassment/Assault Response & Prevention (SHARP) person for me to contact. Sexual assaults, when reported, were often met with retaliation. I was told it would be dealt with through the chain of command, but the officers and senior NCOs upheld the status quo. They acted as if nothing had happened.

In retrospect, I should have seen the provost marshal. There was no commander on my base because it was too small, but another option was the battalion commander in Stuttgart, Germany. This was the first time I had to deal with an adult issue . . . and I had to do it alone.

There was no training for this situation. I did the best I could with what I had at the time. Today, members of the military are educated from day one how to report, where to find the SHARP officer, and how to seek out counseling in the aftermath of sexual harassment or assault. There were no resources available to me.

Upon my discharge, I was informed I was not a veteran and was ineligible for care at the Veterans Administration. Like too many survivors, I was given a re-enlistment code on my DD-214 that translated to me having a personality disorder. This was done without the benefit of any mental health evaluation. I learned many years later that this was common practice for those who reported MST and failed to complete their initial enlistment.

When I joined the military, I intended to complete twenty years. Instead, fourteen short months later, I was back in the civilian world—in my parents' house. I didn't know how to talk to them. I wanted to tell them what had happened, but when I called to inform them that I was getting out of the Army, my father's response was, "Did they catch you using drugs, or did you get pregnant?"

The pride he had in Alabama had turned into utter disappointment. My response was to shut down and shut them out. It was more than ten years before my father and I had another meaningful conversation.

For more than two decades after I left the Army, I suffered with undiagnosed and untreated post-traumatic stress disorder (PTSD). As a result, I had four failed marriages and three children who didn't live with me. I never held a job for more than fourteen months, moved over a dozen times, and was homeless more times than I can count.

A couple months after seeing *The Invisible War,* I found myself at the first Veteran Affairs (VA) Stand Down event for homeless veterans in Daytona Beach, Florida. I wasn't homeless, but I had a fixed income and was struggling to survive from month to month. They typically offered clothes and camping gear to veterans. I was hoping to get a new pair of boots and maybe some BDUs, but I walked out of there with a full rucksack. I received boots, t-shirts, a bed roll, sleeping bag, mess kit (metal plate, cup, and utensils), and a mosquito net/tent. They even gave me bus passes so I could take all my gear home, and I could come back for the free lunch.

After I ate, I was approached by a VA employee. She was doing an after-action report at the exit. She asked me a few questions: Did

I find all the services I was seeking? How could they improve future Stand Down events? Was I enrolled in the VA?

I voiced my opinions, comparing that day to other events of this kind that I had previously attended. I told her I was not enrolled in the VA and told her why. Sometime during the previous two decades, the regulations had changed, so I was encouraged to meet with the MST coordinator. I did, and she started my healing process.

I was given an evaluation that resulted in a PTSD diagnosis. It was strongly suggested that I file a claim to get my PTSD service-connected disability. When I started a claim, I started a battle with the VA for benefits. During this fight, my claim was denied twice. Despite my military service being brief, I did learn how to fight. I obtained a lawyer through the National Veterans Legal Service Project (NVLSP). I tracked down a few people who had served with me and got letters to support my claim.

After six years of fighting for a claim that wasn't even filed until two decades after my discharge, I won! I had enough backpay to purchase my first home, furnish that home, pay down some bills, and repair my credit. I even managed to take a mini vacation!

Although my dreams of military life were cut short, I did take away a few lessons. Two of the most important things I learned are to never give up and that I alone can change my future. There were times I was certain that the proverbial light at the end of the tunnel was nothing more than a train bearing down on me. Somehow, I managed to keep fighting for what was important to me. Eventually I started to see the light was actually the promise of a brighter future. All I needed to do was stand up and keep moving forward. Occasionally I may trip on the tracks. I may even stumble and fall on the rails, but as long as I get back on my feet and keep walking toward the light, I have the ability to do anything I can imagine.

In today's military, sexual harassment and assault are taken more seriously. Every person in uniform is given SHARP program training, and each person filing a report has choices in how that report is going to be handled, which wasn't the case in 1988. These cases are starting to be investigated by outside agencies instead of the direct chain of command. The UCMJ laws that pertain to military personnel have recently made assault/harassment chargeable offenses that have potential prison time attached. Victims are given mental health treatment and counseling and offered the tools they need to become survivors.

Today's military is very different from the Army I served in, but they still have a long way to go.

For far too long, I allowed myself to be overlooked and treated like I was less than those around me. I did everything I could to survive on the fringe. I didn't want to be noticed, because if people didn't see me, they couldn't hurt me. For too many years, I failed to realize that by making myself invisible, I was hurting myself more than anyone else ever could.

Stand up for yourself. Speak your truth. Tell your story.

Above all else, don't let yourself become invisible.

Terri Post resides in Elmira, New York, and has found the therapeutic value of art with regard to PTSD. She enjoys glassblowing and has her work on display at the Honfleur Gallery (Washington, DC), the FDR Library (Hyde Park, NY), the Military Women's Memorial (Arlington, VA), and the Library of Congress (Washington, DC).

Value Added

Reinetta Vaneendenburg, Captain, USN, Retired
August 1979–September 2016

Several months after I had served on a board to select commanders, someone asked me a question that got me thinking. It was drill weekend, and a bunch of reservists were in an office at Norfolk's Reserve Center. A man's voice cut through a lull in the chatter. "Just how did you make captain, Captain?"

Heads turned my way with this question. I looked at the speaker, a lieutenant commander in wrinkled khakis and shaggy hair. He usually had his head buried in a newspaper while I was scurrying around with too much to do, as usual. Still, his question made me stop and think. I only realized later how apropos the question had been in that public setting.

My promotion was a surprise. I had been delighted to don the three stripes of commander and did not anticipate another rank advancement. A colleague from DC called with the news that my name was on the O-6/captain selection message, and I thought she was joking. I have no idea how I made captain. Being selected for promotion to pay grade O-6 is as competitive in the Navy as it is in any branch. Whether it is bird colonel or captain, it's a rare accomplishment.

Hard numbers are difficult to pin down, a result of the Navy's twenty-some different professional communities, each with customized career, retention, and promotion quotas and strategies. The pyramid grows incrementally steeper with each selection wicket.

Admiral or general is the pinnacle of success in the military, but retiring as a commander/lieutenant colonel is considered very respectable.

How did I make captain in the Navy? The only feedback from a selection board is binary: either they loved you (thumbs up) or they hated you (thumbs down). In a Military.com article viewed 16 November 2022, the Navy explained that its "selection boards review the official records of screened members," emphasizing that "board deliberations are not a matter of public record."

A review of my service record with years of fitness reports could have swung the vote either way, since I was on the cusp of naval women line officers allowed to enter its warfare specialties. The selection board could not penalize me for not being warfare-qualified because it was not an available option during my career. This affected the promotion quotas, and some people had difficulty understanding this correction.

I thought back to a presentation—no, it was more of a dialogue—another Navy captain offered to his wardroom of reserve officers two decades ago. He had taken the time to codify key factors to his career, ones he thought contributed to his success. Although he had been an aviator, he highlighted decisions and themes that related to all officers and sailors too. The fact that he cared enough to create this presentation impressed me.

However, I didn't follow most of that captain's suggestions. I didn't select projects that were career enhancing or would put me in contact with high-flyers, fast-trackers, or admirals and the like. I didn't intentionally seek visibility; I published what I felt contributed to the mission of the current command or project. Sometimes that looked like an article in the on-base or local newspaper, sometimes just a photo and a caption. I did not seek training or schoolhouse opportunities because they were geared toward warriors, and I was not one.

I was outspoken and often stood in front of a senior officer getting chewed out. Behavior I considered assertive, the men considered aggressive and therefore inappropriate. I took that to mean they felt threatened by my audacity. Sometimes it was for defending my female colleagues from unwise assignments or ill treatment. For example, the front office knew—because I told them—I was rankled that female officers had to check in and out with the command master chief during my tour at the Navy's San Diego computer center, but male officers didn't.

Other times, my persistence landed me in hot water. I oversaw compiling the Armed Forces Staff College's commemorative book. I avoided its chain of command and submitted drafts of congratulatory letters directly to the staffs of Joint Chiefs of Staff General Shalikashvili and then-President Clinton. The Staff College's general was furious at me for this breach of etiquette when this high-level correspondence was routed back down the chain of command and onto his desk.

However, the letters were signed and formed a distinguished opening of the college's commemorative book. I don't think that would have happened if I had dutifully routed them through the ten or twelve offices on their way up to the Staff College's general and then back down again. Far from being chagrined by the general's scolding, I was delighted that my writing received such an auspicious stamp of approval, for neither top-level staff had edited my input.

Now I was asked for insights on my career. I told him and the other reservists in that crowded room that I was "Value-Added Van," doing more than the task assigned such as writing standard operating procedures for positions or coordinating special events like retirement ceremonies. Before I reported to a new command, I asked my sponsor or point of contact for its organization chart to see who the players were. The command phone book was helpful to match names with jobs and contact info, alleviating asking for such mundane details or avoiding a time-consuming search for something that may or may not be "on the web." I saw my role, regardless of its description, to make my boss's job easier by anticipating needs and providing the information, analysis, or details that person might need. My publications also gave me recognition, especially effective with such an unusual name as mine.

However, my leadership track had stalled inexplicably after a successful tour in charge of a personnel mobilization team. I repeatedly applied for subsequent leadership and other positions using the Navy's personnel assignment system for reserve officers (called the APPLY Program) but never held another pay billet with a reserve unit. Thus, I reverted to an unpaid status that still made me eligible for paid stints, like temporary help or contractors. I could have retired but decided to continue if there were challenging or fun opportunities.

And there were plenty. I spent about a year writing and producing the Armed Forces Staff College's history and designed and established portions of the Navy History and Heritage website. I teamed up with a commander who was a ship driver to invigorate and refine the ground-level Maritime Operations Language School that NATO offered at Newport, Rhode Island's training base. The Navy Inspector General tagged me repeatedly for its inspection teams. I was making more money and enjoying more autonomy than if I had occupied a paid position in a unit.

The lieutenant commander who had posed the question shook his head. I imagine he could not conceive of such a situation where he, as a pilot or ship driver (I don't recall which), didn't make commander, yet I was a "desk jockey" who had been promoted twice over him.

The twist to this exchange was that I had seen his name while I was serving on that selection board, the details of which I could not divulge to him. I looked around the auditorium and saw twenty or thirty senior officers, mostly captains, all men except for me, sitting in an auditorium. The board coordinator was on the stage with the job to ensure the selection process was conducted fairly and per the Navy's sanctioned board rules. The board coordinator explained the precepts for selection: what Big Navy was looking for from this group of candidates.

These guidelines may be vague, such as judging the person's potential for command and resilience. Candidates who were "purple"—having joint service training and experience—or had "time in the sand"—forward deployed to American forces in the Middle East—were to rise to the top of our ranking. "Homesteaders," those who stayed in the same geographic area or job type, were not considered "competitive."

After instructing us on how to use the keypad by our seats, it was time to "calibrate the board." We were shown a series of sample candidates and pressed the buttons. We were the deciders with only three options: promote, continue, or not promote. While these were actual records from people still in service, they were being used as samples and were not in our candidate pool.

After the votes were tallied, the coordinator offered the rationale that drove the previous board's decisions. You could have dropped me with a feather when I realized one of the "not recommended for promotion" examples was the same officer from the Reserve Center, the one who questioned me.

Of course, everything about a selection board, from the moment of acceptance to serve until after the results are published, is a secret. I was sorely tempted to tell this guy that he had been singled out as an example of someone who didn't make the grade. It reminded me of the saying first quoted in the University of Notre Dame's student newspaper in 1898: "You would be rich if you could buy him for what he was worth and sell him for what he thought he was worth."

Junior officers are notorious for believing their personnel evaluations; I can name a dozen officers who wrongly claimed their inevitable rise to flag-officer rank. A lot can go wrong to subvert an auspicious career in those first ten or twenty years. The word on the street was that a naval officer's probability of making admiral was one in two hundred.

Let's consider the roughly 600 ensigns commissioned in 2007. A new officer's initial obligation may be four years, as in my case, or five years (now six) for Academy and ROTC graduates. Not everyone who wants to stay may; of this 600, six were separated for "failure to achieve promotion" and three for misconduct.

Roughly half of first-term officers typically decide to leave. Some turn in their uniforms for better jobs, to attend graduate school, or to train or explore different careers. Naval officers cite family issues as reasons for departure—difficulty finding reliable childcare or deciding to parent full time. Another complaint is the hardship of managing dual careers, despite the Navy's efforts for co-locating. The Navy has revised its thinking about the need to repeatedly move its members around the world. The Navy's first significant manpower wicket is at lieutenant commander (O-4), leaving about 220 of the 600 officers still serving in the active-duty Navy.

The next culling puts about 100 officers on the commander's selection list. Perhaps 30 of those from the original 600 officers next pin on the silver eagle of captain. How many of those 600 just-commissioned ensigns would feel emboldened if told they had a five percent chance of making captain? I know I wouldn't have put money on my horse to win. Promotion is comparable among graduates of Officer Candidate School, ROTC, and the Academy, except for the highest slot of admiral. The Navy Academy at Annapolis provides a tenth of the Navy's new officers but one-half of the Navy admirals.

Like any population followed over time, this cohort in the range of retirement (twenty-year point) traveled a variety of paths upon departure from the service. Many choose to retire when faced with a stalled career, parlaying their military skills to lucrative positions with military contractors or the Civil Service. I saw many reservists retire rather than continue to work for free, which would garner them retirement credit.

How did I make captain? While I was thriving, going from one project to another, my peers were retiring. Maybe there were few of us to choose from in the candidate pool. Maybe I inadvertently waited the competition out. I pinned on captain in October 2001 and retired in 2016 with thirty-six years of service, which included active duty and reserve time.

My career track was haphazard at best, based on my predilections, luck, and the faith of those officers who hired me for special projects. My career path is also not replicable. The Navy ended the sixty-odd-year practice of mandating women officers in the single category as support personnel. Most of the women still serving transitioned to the new human resource or information systems communities. Moreover, the implementation of integrating women into the warfare training and pipeline ensures that, what to me was unassailable, to them is now commonplace.

Women officers who enter the Navy today have a designated path to serve in a warfare or technical community. Even so, there are as many ways to make captain as captains. And my success proves it.

National Endowment for the Arts Military Veteran Fellow Reinetta Van is a regular contributor to The War Horse. *The essay collection* Navy Blues: Between WAVES and Warriors *is under consideration for publishing. The oral history* US Navy Women Line Officers: From Support to Spear Tip *is under contract. The limited-edition* Armed Forces Staff College Fifty-Year Commemorative History *was published in 1996.*

The Difference a Class Makes

Elaine Little, Chief Warrant Officer-2, US Army, Retired
November 1982–August 2008

In January 2004, I received orders for Afghanistan as part of an interrogation unit. After finishing the pre-mobilization period, we were scheduled to reach Afghanistan by early May.

In the interim, we trained: first aid, cultural acclimation, and small unit leadership tactics. There I was on north Fort Hood in the blazing sun, ineptly deploying Army hand signals as we navigated the Texas brush.

At the time, the slogan was "Every Soldier is a Rifleman." This saying applied to me as much as it did to the sergeant in our group who shot out the sideview mirror of a Humvee with his M16 during a tactical driving exercise. He was written up for aiming a weapon loaded with blanks in the direction of soldiers, but he wasn't sent home. In the end, he deployed with the rest of us.

I had a rocky relationship with Army training during my twenty-six-year career. I understood it was effective. I just resented the way they made you learn. Basic training was characterized by constant yelling and humiliation to make you work harder and faster. Later during Advanced Individualized Training, the threat that you might end up at Cook School if you didn't measure up motivated us. I wonder what they told the cooks who weren't passing muster?

I understood the value of yelling and aggressive behavior as an attention-getting technique to get a bunch of confused young people onto the same page as soon as possible. The fear of Cook School was a smart tactic. It wasn't only my subpar cooking skills; if I didn't finish the military school I signed up for, I could kiss goodbye to my $8,000-before-taxes sign-on bonus.

After completing your military occupational specialty, you moved to your duty station. At this point, on-the-job training took over, punctuated with hazing designed to integrate you into a group you weren't even sure you wanted to be a part of. Picture obscene signs pasted to your back and uncomfortable jokes ad nauseum until your trainer judged you capable of doing the job yourself without overt harassment.

Subsequent classes concentrated on maintaining your job performance or reinforcing Army values. They often had a spoon-fed quality, sometimes useful with difficult subjects, but problematic when learning a "soft skill," like concepts related to leadership, for example. There was a way the Army liked you to think and react to things. It made me feel like I wasn't allowed to think independently or question the material, which is why I was so surprised by the required classes during my pre-mobilization period at Fort Hood toward the end of my military career.

I like to think the leadership may have recognized us as adults going to war. I think it's more likely it was one of those happy Army accidents. Nonetheless, the "accident" worked in our favor. We weren't a bunch of kids straight out of high school. In our National Guard unit, the youngest was around twenty-four, the oldest in his fifties. The civilian jobs among us ranged from police officer to housewife to state employee. For the most part, we were a diverse group of intelligent and thoughtful people.

Several classes stood out. First, Combat Lifesaver Class, a forty-hour requirement for troops deploying to combat areas. For a soldier used to National Guard classes consisting of a bored instructor reading word for word off a PowerPoint slide, these classes were a revelation. (Disclaimer: sometimes I was that bored instructor.) The class taught familiar skills like applying bandages, clearing the airway, calling in medical support, and transporting the casualty. This time though, we had to perform as a calm and attentive coach coached us. The type of training I'd been yearning for. There's nothing like having to replicate a task as the instructor talks you through the process.

Bandaging your buddy with a non-existent wound? Not a problem. Place the sterile white gauze in the correct area and you're good. Clear the airway? Place the victim on the side with their mouth open. The side position enables substances like blood, mucus, or vomit to drain out and keeps the tongue from blocking the airway. Easy enough. If we got our victim in the right position and parroted the instructions, we learned and we passed.

Next up, start an IV. A more difficult proposition. We practiced on a dummy plastic arm with the veins drawn in for convenience. This was only the rehearsal for doing a real IV on our buddy using saline solution. Eventually we would penetrate the skin, wielding the needles with careful precision and ensuring the saline drip fed into their veins. I dreaded that part. What if I couldn't find their vein? What if I caused them to bleed?

The first day, we only went as far as the practice arm, but soon we paired up. This directive hurled me back to the grade school playground where I was consistently picked last for dodgeball, kickball, softball, you name it. Even for the spelling bee, which I didn't understand. Why would anyone assume my inability to hit a softball had anything to do with my spelling ability? Anyway, once again, history repeated itself. Nobody wanted to be the pin cushion to my needle.

When the dust settled, I was partnerless until my very nice commander offered to be my victim/subject. I suspected his volunteering to let an obviously nervous, unsure person give him an IV as the kind of good deed that would earn him massive brownie points. When I left the class, I wondered if I could successfully complete the procedure, and more importantly, how I would handle myself under scrutiny as everyone in the class looked on.

The day arrived. I always thought of the commander as unflappable. Today he seemed sweaty and tense. Fortunately, I got his vein on the first try. A miracle. No spilt blood. The needle slid in, and the saline solution pumped through the tubing without a fuss.

Next up, me. I thought I could relax as the commander prepared to plunge the needle into my right arm. Unfortunately, the first poke didn't do it. Nor did the second or third. I, who had been staring at the classroom wall, aimed my eyes discreetly downward to see what the heck was going on, hoping he got this done in under ten tries. Finally. The needle was placed.

"Hmm, veins were a little hard to see," he mused in his aw-shucks way.

I'd never been told that before. I let it go. Strange. The whole experience made me feel more confident and also made me question my own negative opinions.

The next phase of training centered on politics, culture, and history. Many of us hadn't tackled a history class since high school, and suddenly we landed in "American History from an Anti-American Perspective." The title of the class sounded subversive. In reality, it was more like the facts presented weren't carefully edited to only strain out examples that flattered America. I was pleasantly surprised the Army contracted a class where the instructor's primary source was Howard Zinn's, *A People's History of the United States.*

The saying "history is written by the winners" was never so clear as when listening to the interpretation of American history espoused by Zinn. The instructor began the class by saying, "History is as much about the facts you leave in as the facts you leave out."

The course made me feel the Army was treating me like an adult who could appreciate and understand complicated political ideologies and how they sometimes can be misused depending on who's in charge. Great training for interrogators. We already knew we had a dubious reputation since the news in the spring of 2004 was thick with the Abu Ghraib scandal.

We supplemented the politics with lessons on Afghanistan culture, language, and religion. All was good until we got to the language part, where we learned simple Arabic words and phrases. Good to know . . . except our destination was Afghanistan where Dari and Pashto were the common languages. Oh well. It was still early in the war. When people encountered us on post, they assumed we would go to Iraq.

Then came religious study. The indepth explanations of the different sects in Islam, like the Sunni and the Shia, made Islam much more relatable. In some countries, the Shia were in power, in others, the Sunni. To me, it sounded something like the Protestants and the Catholics in Northern Ireland. The religion classes especially pulled me out of my Christian-centered mindset and reinforced the concept that God is present throughout the world. Every religion, including my own, has committed great sin as well as great good. All invaluable lessons to interrogators who needed to understand the mindset of the Afghan people. Interrogation often depended on finding common ground with the person you were interrogating. How could one expect to question people if you couldn't comprehend their beliefs and culture?

My takeaway from my experience with military training is it's integral to keeping the force ready. It's important, however, that the training evolves as the soldier matures. The goal should be to build and expand upon already-learned concepts, coming at them from a more mature angle in an attempt to make the soldier think, consider, learn, and advance in their grasp of the subject.

The classes I attended in the runup to my Afghanistan deployment were examples of this. A fitting circumstance since my unit was being deployed to a war zone and thrust into positions of danger and great responsibility.

Elaine Little lives in Los Angeles where she works as a homeless veterans outreach coordinator at the Veterans Benefit Administration. She writes fiction, essays, and scripts and is working on a short story collection. Her publishing credits include pieces in Consequence Forum, The War Horse, Proud to Be, Volumes 10 and 11, *and the acclaimed anthology* Powder: Writing by Women in the Ranks from Vietnam to Iraq.

Letter to a Deploying Soldier

Tanya Whitney, Master Sergeant, US Army, Retired
March 1983–July 2010

"Hurry up and wait" echoes in your mind as you stand in the queue ready to board the transport. It's eerily silent, with no talking or laughing. Some heads hang low while others twist around with uncertain stares as the line slowly moves forward. The sun beats down on the concrete. The heat radiates and adds to the misery. The smell of jet fuel permeates the air.

As someone who was once in the same position, here are a few words of wisdom.

I wished someone had talked to me before my first deployment, so I would have been prepared. To give you a bit of advice on what you might expect, I am writing this letter. Hopefully, it will impart the things I learned to better prepare you.

You're anxious, fearful, and probably ready to cry. You're not alone. Everyone sitting on the plane around you feels the same way. Fear is often considered a negative emotion. However, fear actually helps keep us safe with the ability to cope with danger. You're probably feeling as though you won't return. That thought hangs in the back of everyone's mind. It's a natural response to the unknown world you're marching into. Even the most seasoned soldier feels that no two missions are identical. Stay aware—that flight or fight instinct will keep you alive as long as you listen to it.

The world you know will never be the same. You are embarking on a mission that will change the very fiber of your soul. Go with

102

it; don't try to fight the change. This is a life experience no different than any you would have at home. There are many lessons we only understand by facing certain situations. The world is a dangerous place no matter where you are. Now the danger is going to be right in your face. Learn from it and become stronger in the end. You've been training for this; put it to use.

Write, call, email, or whatever you can do, as often as you can. It's important to keep yourself in touch with the folks in your support channels. It will be a strong protective factor in your mental health while deployed. Your family loves you and wants to know how you are. No, don't tell them the details of your mission, how many you or your buddies killed, or how many of your buddies were killed or wounded. Deep, emotional exchanges are not required. Talk about your pets, the weather, or even your crazy relatives (we all have at least one). They just need to know you are alive and well. Not hearing from you is worse than knowing you are in a combat zone.

Keep your head low and your weapon at the ready. Be prepared for anything; expect the worst. Doing so will keep you aware and on your toes. Have options for the unexpected; luck can only take you so far. Complacency kills, especially soldiers in combat. It's not good to completely relax in an environment where you won't be able to tell friend from foe. By expecting the worst, you won't be surprised at the outcome.

You're going to a place where culture, habits, values, and language will be vastly different. You will likely be as foreign to them. Good manners and politeness are always appropriate when dealing with the general population. Be respectful. You are representing our country, so make a good impression. Avoid discussions of politics, religion, and human rights, just to name a few issues that may exacerbate an already tenuous situation. Even in America, these topics can create conflict.

Sleep when you can and while you can. It's going to be in short supply. The body and mind need time to rest. When you're exhausted, your body can put you to sleep. Should this happen at the wrong time . . . well, let's just say, it might not be good. Also, your mind needs rest to better adapt to input. A lack of sleep makes you feel foggy and impacts your thought process. A cat nap during the day will do wonders for your physical and mental health.

Oh yeah! I'm sure you didn't pack any but find a bottle of ketchup or hot sauce to keep with you. It's the only thing that will make Meals-Ready-to-Eat for three meals a day edible after the first week. As with sleep, sustenance is also important. Declining to eat is not something to do. You need the calories and energy. As I mentioned before, stay in touch with family and friends. It's the best way to request care packages with real food, especially small packages of food that can be carried with you during travel. Stock up when and where you can. Even when you get something you may not like to eat or use, keep it. The barter economy is alive and doing very well in deployed locations, especially those areas where access to the post exchange is limited. Money becomes useless when there's nowhere to spend it, but a shortage of usable goods drives up the value of many items in a remote area.

I think that's all for now. Your head is probably spinning and trying to take all this in. Regardless of where you end up, make the best of it. Bad attitudes only make time pass slowly. So good luck and Godspeed.

P.S. Even if you aren't a religious person, take the pocket Bible the chaplain offers to you. It makes for good reading while you're sitting around waiting. There will be plenty of that. Keep it in your left breast pocket. It might just save your life, figuratively and literally.

After retiring, Tanya Whitney returned to Sorrento, Louisana, with her husband and two children. Since returning home, she has volunteered with several local veterans' groups serving the community. She is the head coach for the St. Amant High School Gators Cross Country team and serves as an assistant track and field coach for St. Amant High.

Could Be Worse

Beth Liechti, Colonel, US Army, Retired
May 1981–July 2009

Most spring days in northern Illinois start cold and raw. Today peaks sunny and warm. I hitch a ride to Boomer's Mile High Club, an airstrip in the cornfields near Hinckley. After two hours of "do this" and "don't do that," I harness up in a sport parachute and board a six-seater Cessna 180. At two thousand feet, the jump instructor motions me to climb out on the strut of the wing. Up here, fear is as far from me as the ground when I push away from the plane and into the wind. Jumping triggers a hunger for more height to find ground enough to hold me.

I'm ready.

Two months later, my college freshman year ends. I move in with Mom during summer break.

"Do you really have to go?" she asks. "What if you break an arm or a leg, or worse?"

"No doubt," I reply while checking my bag.

"Well, if your mind's made up, be careful." Then she asks, "Aren't you scared?"

She means well, but her words fill my nineteen-year-old, know-it-all self with fight.

"Mom, I signed a contract. I have orders to report tomorrow. I've been training almost a year. Of four cadets selected this year, I'm the second female from our school to ever attend."

I turn and look at her. "You should be proud of me."

More than scared, nerves crisscross my ego, accusing me of not training enough. Falling out of a run or returning home without silver jump wings looms larger than fear. An injury isn't even considered. Youth, my ally and adversary. I'm a young woman with a big chip on my shoulder headed for Airborne (paratrooper) training: an Army school that only five years earlier, in 1974, had opened to females.

I look out the window and see my father pull up in an old, yellow Toyota to drive me to O'Hare airport. If he's bothered about my destination, he doesn't say and only wishes me well.

Two jet plane rides and I arrive in Columbus, Georgia, "Fountain City" on the banks of the Chattahoochee. First time I've traveled south of the Mason-Dixon Line. Late day Georgia heat slaps me awake as I inhale thick southern air. Fresh vanilla pine mingles with magnolias. At the airport, I catch a cab to post with two other troopers—both guys. They don't say much to me, nor I to them.

At the front gate, the sign shows, "Welcome to Ft. Benning — U.S. Army."

Once on post, the cab stops in front of the 44th Student Company barracks. I survey the three-story, U-shaped, cement block building. Institutional but home for the next three weeks. A sidewalk extends from the street to the middle of the building.

I follow the other two troopers on the duffle bag drag to the orderly room and notice several guys hanging out of the windows. They yell and wave as we walk down the middle of the U.

First time I've run a gauntlet of gawkers. I'm not sure what to do. My instinct is to yell back, but I don't.

"Hey, baby, I've been waitin' all my life for you," one guy moans. Another guy yells, "Come to daddy."

Halfway to the orderly room, more guys appear on both sides of the building, yelling and making rude gestures. The two troopers walking with me increase the distance between them and me. So much for the buddy system. At first caught off-balance, I then rally. These guys, my future fellow trainees, are trying too hard to get my attention. I resist and keep my eyes focused straight ahead. They'll need to do better. I grew up between three brothers. I knew how to take jabs from fellow cadets and how to give them back.

"Hey, lil' beaver, lemme show you my big dog," growls another guy. "I'd love to wrap your long brown hair round my big dog."

As I walk by dog boy's window, he starts barking, deep and slow. I smile. What a goofball he was.

A chorus of cussing and catcalls welcomes me to the renowned US Army Infantry School on May 31, 1979.

Could be worse.

Ft. Benning is the second Army post I've ever entered and my first experience with active-duty Army training. Now I'm known as "CW2," which is stenciled on masking tape on the front of my steel pot (helmet): "C" for charlie (cadet), "W" for whiskey (woman), "2" for second cadet woman. My place is front row, fourth man, first stick (the line up in the aircraft), second platoon. Knowing my place helps as I try to fit in.

When I get to the right spot at the right time in the right uniform, the "black hats" yell at someone else to drop (to do push-ups). Our instructors—all enlisted men, mostly sergeants—are known as black hats because they wear black baseball caps emblazoned with their rank and airborne badge, black tees, and starched OD (olive drab—the Army's favorite color) fatigue pants. Black hats scream and curse.

"Drop, Airborne!" they yell first to one then another trainee.

Constant screaming reminds me of growing up when my father frequently hollered to keep us five kids in line.

"Fall in!" yells First Sergeant, a white guy with biceps as thick as my thighs.

More than 300 troopers scramble on loose gravel to line up at attention on the cables. Maybe twenty-five of us are females.

The pace of the first day lumbers as we in-process. Standing at parade rest for a couple hours, I try to follow lectures on fraternization, personal hygiene, and helmet safety. The colonel drones on. Under my steel pot, Georgia sun heats up my head. I flash back to the scruffy mess sergeant who grinned as he scooped hot grits onto my tray that morning. I thought it was cream of wheat. My gut churns and I throw up. I'm in the front rank, so no one is in the line of fire. Muffled laughter erupts behind me. I run to the back of formation and heave until there's nothing left. Surely the black hats will send me packing.

"Okay, Charlie Whiskey Two, you finished with breakfast? Move out!" yells a black hat. "Beat feet before I drop you."

Cadre decide it was nerves and allow me to continue. Was it grits or nerves? After the first day, the training days rush by from wake up to lights out. I keep the pace and don't drop out of the four-mile airborne shuffles, double-time runs that finish each morning's physical training session. After each run, I join my airborne buddies for a smoke break.

The training during week one—Ground Week—was run long, hard, and hot.

On the third evening, Denise, my roommate, reclines on her bunk, fussing and fidgeting over stuff and guys of no consequence. From appearances, Denise looks in control. She knows how to work the black hats, catching cushy details like filling out duty rosters instead of cleaning the laundry room like me.

"Hey, lil' miss soldier," Denise calls out, loud enough so others can hear as our door is open. "Maybe you wanna shine my boots?" Giggling. "Whad ya say? Come ooonnn."

Aren't we girls supposed to stick together? I nod and continue shining my boots. I don't think Denise is serious about finishing the course. However, I am. I have much to prove. She mumbles, then trips out of the room.

Later that week, word travels that John Wayne died. Troopers trade memories of The Duke. Training continues. After fifty or sixty tries, I want nothing more to do with jumping or landing, whether from a platform, the swing landing trainer, or the thirty-four-foot tower. I hurt all over and I'm mad: mad at the black hats, mad at my airborne buddies, and mad at the Georgia heat and sand. I'm also concerned. Anyone caught limping is recycled. The pain from shin splints in my right leg grows, probably from running in combat boots on the hardball (gravel) roads. I must ignore it.

I push hard until mid-afternoon on Friday of week one when my spirit deflates.

"Drop, Airborne!" yells a tall, thin black hat. "You, Charlie Whiskey Two. Get down!"

Breaking the rules, like running too slow or talking out of turn, means pushing Georgia to Florida wherever I stand, concrete, gravel, or grass. In this instance, I wiped sweat from my brow when at the position of parade rest. Some black hats favor "beat your boots," the military version of deep knee bends or squats. Face down in the front-leaning rest position, my sweaty palms slip in red clay.

"Airborne," he screams, "did you hear me? I said give me ten push-ups. One. Two. Three. Four. Five. Six. Six. Six. . . naawww, Airborne. Try again, Airborne."

My airborne buddies stare at me. Steel pot, wet fatigues, and wool socks sizzle my insides from my head to my gut. My breath comes in short gulps. Biceps scream in pain. Legs shake. Torso dips. Inside I repeat to myself, take it an hour at a time—if an hour is too long, thirty minutes, five minutes, and in the front-leaning rest position, one minute at a time. Finally, I knock out ten good ones.

"Okay. Airborne, get back in line," he yells. "Don't do it again or you'll bolo like the leg you are. Move out, Airborne. Move."

As the black hat walks toward the others, he mutters, "Ya know I love you, Airborne. I love all ya Airborne troopers. Just making sure you don't break your necks."

A couple guys snort. I believe him. Maybe I'll stick it out.

Could be worse.

At the end of the day, back at the barracks, I learn my roommate, lil' miss Denise, fell out of a second run.

In the evenings after chow, I iron creases in my fatigues and spit-shine a mirror reflection on my black combat boots. Sometimes I cheat and dab a little Future floor wax on the tips, making sure I'm ready for the next day's inspection. I have no intention of joining the dumbasses in the gig pit. If you don't meet standards, wrong uniform or boots not polished, the black hats send you to the gig pit, where you do extra push-ups or beat-your-boots while everyone else takes a smoke break.

By Tuesday of week two—Tower Week—my roommate departs for home. For reasons unknown to me, she didn't recycle (start the course over from day one). After she leaves, no one watches as I polish my boots in the three-person room.

By Friday, happy to have made it past the 250-foot-tower drop, troopers poke and jab, provoking the black hats to yell at them for pushups. The worst moment occurs. First Sergeant announces cuts and recycles. I bite my lip. Charlie Whiskey 2 is not called. I can continue on to Jump Week, the last week of training.

That evening, the black hats cook burgers and dogs. Everyone shows up in civies. A boom box plays rock and roll. Guys and a few gals dance on the gravel. My airborne brothers grab close looks at my light blue capris but hold their tongues. A welcome change from the first day I walked the gauntlet of catcalls into the barracks. Guess I have proven myself. First Sergeant smiles. That's unusual.

Back in my room before lights out, I lie on my rack with the OD-wool blanket, rubbing Ben Gay over exhausted arms, legs, and chest. Red welts from canopy straps pinching after countless exits from the thirty-four-foot tower cross both sides of my neck. Black and blue marks bisect my chest from punching the quick release on the parachute harness. Purple trails streak along the top of each leg where canvas leg straps dig. Shin splints restrict my right leg. A pulled muscle in my left arm triceps stings. While I'll tough out the last week, the prospect of five jumps intimidates.

Could be worse.

Early on Monday of week three—Jump Week—the company airborne shuffles a mile to Lawson Army Airfield. For my first Infantry School jump, I suit up in a T-10 parachute for a Hollywood jump (no rucksack or rifle). Hobbling to the runway, I'm overcome with the weight and the heat. Bizarre sensations tumble in my stomach while loading onto the C-141 Starlifter jet. When running in formation, a jody (a cadence we sing to keep everyone in step), now buzzes in my head.

> C-130 rolling down the strip.
> Airborne troopers on a one-way trip.
> Mission unspoken, destination unknown.
> Don't even know if they'll ever come home.

Will I come home?

Even with earplugs, the noise surrounding the aircraft deafens. Roar, thrust, and lift off. Flying nape of the earth, up, down, down, up, down. More than jumping or landing, I fear puking. The rule is troopers jump with their bag of puke. A few troopers puke. Within minutes, sympathetic pukers start hurling. Relieved, Dramamine keeps me puke-free.

Jump door opens. Wind roars. My fifth time ever flying in a jet. Six minutes from the drop zone. Jumpmaster shouts the series of jump commands and gives hand signals. After the "Check Equipment" command, each trooper must yell "Okay" and slap the guy in front of them. The guy behind me hauls off with enthusiasm, almost lifting me off the floor. I try the same to the guy in front of me but with less success. I don't think he even notices.

Green light blinks ON. The Air Force drops paratroopers from an elevation of 1,000 to 1,200 feet, which matters little when you're shuffling up to the open door of a jet plane cruising at 125–135 knots. With my yellow static line in hand, I tug my helmet strap, sweating as sensations escalate to somersaults in my gut. The line of troopers mashes close together. The guys in front of me disappear out the open door.

At the door, the jumpmaster yells, "Go!" and slaps me on the butt. I take one step, and in an instant, my body is sucked out of the C-141. No time to change my mind. A hot jet blast hits me. I tuck, head down, hands on reserve, feet and knees together. My body jolts but doesn't hurt as the opening shock of the static line pulls the chute out.

Opening my eyes, I see the back end of the aircraft flying away. I look up and see line twists. Pulling them apart, I slip left and drift down as a delicious silence, interrupted by gentle breezes, rustles through my canopy. No one yells at me up here. To my left and right, a line of canopies dot the sky as troopers float to earth. I want to look down but don't want to experience "ground rush," so I keep my eyes on the horizon.

Still, I instinctively reach for the ground with my boots. Suddenly, I hit: feet, butt, and push-up muscle, then roll. Not exactly a textbook, five-point parachute landing fall. My chute crumples around my body. I lay for a precious moment, looking up. Doesn't get better than this little patch of Fryar Drop Zone paradise. Much later, I learned the field was named for Private Elmer E. Fryar, 511th Parachute Infantry Regiment, who was awarded the Medal of Honor from action in the Philippine Islands during World War II. By the time seven bullet holes in his chest and stomach ended his life, Fryar had killed twenty-seven Japanese enemies, saving many fellow soldiers.

After packing my chute into the kit bag, I heave the load over my head and double-time across the sand. Despite the weight, it still feels like I'm floating under a canopy.

On Thursday, the day of my final school jump, I celebrate my twentieth birthday, dropping from a C-123 propeller aircraft under an MC-1B chute with a rucksack and M16A1 rifle. In four days, I have walked away from all five jumps: two Hollywood, one night, and two combat equipment. I feel invincible.

On Friday, my last day in Georgia, the June morning rises steamy. Standing toward the back of the cavernous Infantry Hall, I can barely see the stage, shoulder to shoulder with three hundred thirty-seven men and thirteen women. For a year, I've been chasing this moment.

"Airborne is a state of mind," thunders the general.

A young black hat walks to my front. I don't know him. My eyes fix on his nameplate: Sergeant Walker. He pins the wings over the left breast pocket on my fatigues. Clumsy, he tries not to offend. The moment turns awkward. Much as I strive to fit in, I'm not one of the guys. After he moves away, I peek. The silver jump wings are crooked but still I smile.

Graduation concludes and our company forms in the street. Puffed out, jaunty, and singing loudly, we march back to the company area. For the final time, a formation of new airborne troopers lines up on the cables.

First Sergeant announces mail call. The orderly room sergeant steps to the microphone and starts calling names. Standing at parade rest in the front rank, the heat, sun, and humidity that threatened me for the last three weeks seems hardly noticeable.

The sergeant holds up a white envelope. He's calling, "Charlie Whiskey Two! Charlie Whiskey Two!"

I step back out of rank, rush to the end of formation, and scramble to the front behind the First Sergeant. With my eyes on the envelope, I miscalculate and trip over the mic cord, falling face first into the gravel as the entire company watches.

A black hat yells, "Stay on down, Airborne, and knock me out ten for old times' sake!"

Hoots and hollers from my airborne brothers and sisters echo off the barracks walls as I crank them out. I grin from ear to ear.

Could be worse.

Beth Liechti volunteers as a coach/editor with Military Experience and the Arts and teaches "Launch Your Light," a journal writing course. Her poetry and stories have been published in LOA–Line of Advance, As You Were: The Military Review, Cactus Wren-dition, *and the* Mighty Pen Project Anthology.

Proud to Have Served

Dawn Brotherton, Colonel, USAF, Retired
December 1988–October 2016

When people thank me for my service, I used to feel like an imposter. I didn't join the military for any noble notion of wanting to serve my country; it was my job. Many veterans gave a lot for their country. It wasn't a sacrifice for me; however, I made the commitment and signed a four-year contract.

I served twenty-eight years in the Air Force, beginning during the Cold War and retiring as a colonel while we were still sending troops to Afghanistan and Iraq, but at no time was my life threatened in combat. Even while deployed in support of Operation Allied Force for Kosovo, after my sixteen-hour shift, I slept snuggly in a hotel in southern Italy.

I started as a Minuteman II missile launch officer, a position not highly sought after in the Air Force, but I needed the Reserve Officers' Training Corps scholarship to pay for college. People have a million questions about what it was like to be in the position of potentially ending the world as we know it. First, I want to point out that a key turn was required, not a button push. And no, there was no way a crew could go rogue and plunge the world into a nuclear holocaust.

Honestly, I didn't think about going to war. I didn't believe it would ever come to that. Most of the time, my crew partner and I traded sleep shifts in the underground capsule during our twenty-four-hour rotation. When we weren't eighty feet underground, we studied codes, drilled on potential launch scenarios, practiced deciphering launch messages, and went about our lives.

When choosing my next assignment, I volunteered for the Republic of Korea as a personnel officer, because I heard I'd get my choice of a follow-on assignment, and I really wanted to go to Europe. I had only been out of the United States once before, so Korea opened my eyes. Whiteman Air Force Base in Missouri only housed the missile wing at that time; Osan Air Base in the Republic of Korea was my introduction to airplanes and the fighter pilot community.

At Osan, we participated in monthly exercises where we donned our gas masks and chemical suits, complaining about how uncomfortable we were the whole time. Imagine being put out by something that would save our lives in the case of an attack. We were missing the point.

I eventually made it to Germany as an executive officer and reveled in the beauty of the European countryside, traveling every chance I got. Work was something I did between weekend getaways. I sloughed through paperwork, kept my group commander on schedule so he could fly, and ensured everyone crossed their Ts and dotted their Is.

When I transitioned into the inspector general's office, I wrote exercise scenarios to test the wing's readiness to deploy. The closest I came to danger was when I simulated a plane crash or terrorist invasion of the base. Even in that, I was on the outside, grading the wing's response.

As the chief of staff for the 40th Expeditionary Operations Group to Gioia del Colle in southern Italy, I ensured smooth operations at the deployed location, interacted with the Italian base commander, and tracked the comings and goings of all military personnel. The days were long and never boring, but all the while, I listened to the war stories told by the pilots returning from their missions over Kosovo.

As I bounced up the ranks, moving from one job to the next without a specific plan, I always did my best and sought out new challenges, but I viewed the Air Force as my job. The Department of

Defense was just my employer. I didn't feel particularly brave when I went to the office each day to sort out personnel issues and sit on promotion panels. As an assignments officer in San Antonio, Texas, I enjoyed helping others progress in their careers, trying to match the desire of the individual with the needs of the Air Force. People don't appreciate how important their records are until they are preparing for a promotion board.

When I tell people I was a NATO staff officer, they envision that I shared deep, dark secrets with foreign countries. I picture the times I huddled with officers from Italy, Spain, Germany, and others at the picnic benches as we nervously prepared for our presentation to the NATO committee. Our focus was on not looking stupid in front of our bosses, not the fate of democracy.

Even when I became a unit commander at Naval Station Norfolk, my job was to prepare my troops to deploy and, once on the ground, grow into the foundation of a rapidly mobilized headquarters staff. We didn't deploy as an entire unit, and I was never placed in danger. As airmen and soldiers boarded the planes headed for Crimea and Liberia, I put on my air battle uniform and went to the office. I felt like a phony. They were the real heroes.

My last assignment at the Pentagon in Washington, DC, was probably the diciest. There is a certain level of danger anytime a military person approaches Capitol Hill, where Congress holds the authority to determine the amount of funding the Armed Forces receive. One miscalculated word to the wrong person can have unintended consequences. As a legislative liaison, I often escorted general officers to the Hill to meet with members of Congress or their staff. I was a background player, not in the spotlight. But when I had to accompany twenty-five-year-old congressional staffers on their boondoggles to military bases on the Department of Defense's dime, I had to bite my tongue when they ordered the most expensive thing on the menu from the nicest civilian restaurants just because they could. Hurting their feelings could result in a bad report to their representative which, in turn, could mean a nay vote on an Air Force initiative.

When I look back on my military career, I'm not sure what I would have done differently. I went where I was assigned without complaint. I never once refused to deploy or to risk my life. My performance reports and promotions reflect achievements above and beyond the average. There isn't a check box that says, "Was never put in danger" (although that can become a tipping point during promotion boards).

My duties had to be accomplished so that troops could respond to the nation's call. If no one did the work to in-process them to the base or train them to do their job efficiently and effectively, the airmen's lives could be in danger. If no one tracked their movements at a forward operating base or ensured their pay was straight so their families back home were taken care of while the airmen focused on the enemy, the mission could fail. If Congress wasn't constantly reminded of the need for military funding, they would surely find even more budget cuts that could undermine our deployers and thus our national security.

It took many years and a lot of growing up for me to realize that one doesn't have to put themself in harm's way to be a hero; they just have to be willing to do their part for the mission to succeed.

Now when people thank me for my service, I've learned to say, "I'm proud to have served."

Dawn Brotherton is an award-winning author of eighteen books and featured speaker at writing and publishing seminars. When writing, she draws on her experience in the military as well as her time as a softball coach and Girl Scout leader. Her variety of interests has led to a range of genres including mystery, romance, young adult fantasy, middle grade sports, picture book, and nonfiction.